The
Tenderloin District of San Francisco
Through Time

THE
TENDERLOIN DISTRICT OF SAN FRANCISCO
THROUGH TIME

PETER M. FIELD

FONTHILL

Fonthill Media Inc.
www.fonthillmedia.com
office@fonthillmedia.com

First published 2018

ISBN 978-1-63499-092-9

Typeset in Mrs Eaves XL Serif Narrow
Printed and bound in England

Acknowledgments

The idea and support for this book came from longtime Tenderloin resident and activist David Baker. Not only did he contribute substantially towards the production costs of this volume, but he also donated key portions of his collection of Tenderloin archival material, including his file of back issues of the *Tenderloin Times*. In addition to these valuable aids, he also offered anecdotes and memories of the politics of the Tenderloin from the 1970s through today, as well as encouragement and support during the writing of this book. This volume is dedicated to him.

Special thanks are due to my longtime editor and friend Therese Van Wiele, a professional in every sense of the word, who is as skilled in the diplomacy of conveying suggestions to writers as she is in editing text.

Acknowledgements for the use of the many images in the book are in the text. Most scans and permissions were given gratis and the author deeply appreciates the donors' generosity. Special thanks are due to Jacob Schurman, who gave hours of anecdotes and views of family archives, as well as copies of several photographs to flesh out the Wilson family history. In addition, author and collector Glenn Koch generously shared a number of images from his extensive collection which appear in this book. Finally, Chris Carlsson of Foundsf contributed several images as well as generously spending time teaching the author the basics of acquiring the machine this text was written on, as well as dealing with some of its vagaries. There were many others too numerous to list who shared stories, anecdotes, and images over the years. The author gratefully acknowledges these contributions. Any errors are, of course, the author's alone.

INTRODUCTION

When most people remember the Tenderloin's history, they're thinking of the decade-and-a-halves both before and after the 1906 earthquake and fire, when it was famous as the city's upscale hotel, entertainment, and vice district. Yet, it was also democratic. It had something for almost anyone as long as they had the money or projected the illusion of having it.

A sailor fresh off a cruise, a harvest gypsy returning to the city to rest up, a South of Market working stiff, or a petty criminal who lived on the waterfront all went to the Barbary Coast, South of the Slot, Chinatown, Dupont and Morton streets, or other low-priced districts to get drunk on nickel schooners of steam or lager beer and cheap whiskey, throw dice, or play nickel-and-dime poker or faro, and get a woman at one of the cribs or cow yards that infested these areas. After 1906, if you were a slummer, you could go to one or two of the Pacific Street dives that had balconies from where you could drink and watch ... but not mingle.

But a clerk, a business owner, an executive, or a professional who lived north or west of Market Street started with the saloons along the cocktail route until you landed in the Tenderloin for a dinner and an assignation at a French restaurant or found a card game in one of the clubs on Powell or Mason streets or visited one of the parlor houses to round out the evening or went to one of the bathing establishments to take some steam and sober up before going home to your fuming wife. An attendee at a lodge fete—the larger fraternal organizations had headquarters in the Tenderloin or Lower Nob Hill—might hit the saloons, restaurants, or parlor houses before going home to the aforementioned wife. A tourist who came to Frisco "to see the elephant" did all of the above except the cocktail route, of which the out-of-towner was probably ignorant. And the owner of a Tenderloin gambling club, saloon, theater, or restaurant made the rounds of these places every evening and sometimes joined the businessmen in the steam baths before returning to whatever nearby hotel he called home.

For the working man, the Tenderloin also had less expensive concert halls and live shows on the edges of the district and was considered a step up to something a little classier than the Barbary Coast. There was everything from dancing and drinking with so-called "pretty waiter girls" in basement concert halls to variety shows and legitimate theaters. The Wigwam and the Olympia theaters were for the man on the street, while the more pretentious Tivoli, Orpheum, and other playhouses were for everyone, depending on which part of the house they could afford to sit in.

There were also less expensive restaurants and clubs. A Tenderloin card dealer, bartender, bouncer, musician, waiter, or a pretty waiter girl also did the rounds. A petty criminal who used the Tenderloin as a base of operations checked the joints each day and evening, both for pleasure and opportunities, like an inebriated lodge member waiting to be mugged or have his pockets picked, or a sucker who could be conned into a crooked gambling game, or a man looking for a good time who could be slipped a mickey, usually whiskey with knockout drops consisting of either chloral hydrate or tincture of opium—and then rolled.

But the Tenderloin's favorite customer was the legendary "good thing" who occasionally wandered into the neighborhood looking for a debauch. These were scions of wealthy families, remittance men, and errant royalty from other nations. Sometimes more than one of these categories fit the same individual. Others were men who were flush with their latest score: embezzlers, confidence men (who should have known better), thieves, beneficiaries of wills, and others not so easily classified. They all had two things in common: they wanted to go on an extended tear and they had the money to pay for it.

That's the Tenderloin's history that most people think about.

But, the Tenderloin has another more recently acquired history as part of San Francisco's main remaining inner-city poverty pocket. In it are chronically homeless street persons, petty and not so petty criminals, drug and alcohol addicts, the chronically medically and mentally ill, poor people of all ages, refugees, social workers and social activists with their churches and programs, run-down buildings, rehabilitated and subsidized hotels and apartment buildings, dive bars, corner liquor stores, and beat cops. Alongside these are the harbingers of development and gentrification: ethnic restaurants, artists, art galleries, boutiques, and clubs and bars catering to a younger, hip, and upwardly mobile crowd. All are trying to get started with the help of depressed real estate values and rents. And nibbling at the edges are the developers, looking to assemble big money projects.

That's the Tenderloin's recent history that most people think about.

Yet, the Tenderloin's history is vastly richer and more complex than these two versions would have one believe. It was originally a small hamlet in the sand dunes, which became a prosperous and largely conservative Republican neighborhood of single-family houses and mansions. Then, the east half of the area transitioned into the hotel, entertainment, and vice district described above. What residential housing remained became more or less respectable working-class homes, while the west half's middle and upper-class colony of family homes held on until the 1906 earthquake and fire. The entire area was rebuilt over the next twenty-plus years into a hotel and apartment district, along with the entertainment and vice that had already made it famous.

The restrictions of World War I drove vice underground, though this partially resurfaced during Prohibition. The loosening of moral constraints during the Roaring Twenties made the impossible possible when the secretive nature of speakeasies provided a platform on which to open saloons and clubs that admitted women, homosexuals, lesbians, and drag queens.

After repeal, police and politicians tolerated a few of the latter venues because they took cruisers away from Union Square and its shopping district, so that over the next three decades San Francisco's first homosexual quarter grew in the neighborhood's southeast corner, later moving to its western edge, and still later moving back to the southeast corner, before mostly abandoning the neighborhood for the more residential Castro District.

Fiscally, the demand for live entertainment had been one of the primary supports of the Tenderloin's economy since the 1880s, even though the neighborhood suffered from neglect during the Great Depression, and only partially recovered with the boom times of World War II and the Korean War. After this, the loss of Bay Area military bases and their servicemen, the loss of Bay Area war industries and their employees, the increasing expense of producing live entertainment, the growing dominance of the movie industry and its eventual move away from downtown and into the neighborhoods, the advent of better-quality home sound systems, and the development of television and rock and roll pretty much eliminated the demand for live entertainment in the Tenderloin. In addition, post-World War II businesses moved their manufacturing, transportation, and shipping operations away from the expensive land and labor costs of cities. This kind of work had kept even the marginally employable employed, but it was replaced with white collar enterprises that sought employees from a narrower range of the population.

Then there was constantly increasing inflation, especially after the mid-1970s, with the value of wages and private and public benefits falling further and further behind the cost of living. Redevelopment demolished cheap but affordable housing or replaced it with more expensive housing. At the same time, the number of indigents increased with the closing of state institutions for those unable to care for themselves. There was also a growing epidemic of drug and alcohol addicts who were also unable to support themselves. Because of inflation, benefits to keep these unfortunates housed and fed failed to keep pace. While the percentages of the population represented by these groups may have stayed more or less the same, population growth ensured that their numbers increased.

All these circumstances caused a massive influx of various kinds of indigents into the neighborhood, one of the last places in San Francisco to still offer cheap housing. This pushed out the existing residents, who were a mix of workers and retired seniors on limited incomes. Then inflation reached the point where very limited incomes no longer paid for a full month's housing, however transient it may have been. The end result was less adequate resources for increasing numbers of poor people which led to mass homelessness. All these factors had profound impacts on the Tenderloin that are still highly visible today.

At the same time, the tech economy moved into San Francisco's Mid-Market area and triggered yet another wave of development that once again accelerated increases in the cost of living in the Tenderloin, largely because its real estate was still relatively inexpensive when compared to other downtown locations. It also made it a destination of sorts and small trendy storefront businesses began displacing older neighborhood businesses that couldn't afford the rent increases landlords were suddenly demanding.

Where did this all begin?

ONE

FROM SAND DUNES TO NEIGHBORHOOD

When the foundation for the San Francisco Center at Market and Fifth streets was excavated in the 1980s—at what used to be the eastern end of the valley that was one of the Tenderloin's original geographic features—a shell midden was unearthed, a dump used by the area's aboriginal inhabitants around 100 BCE and again around 120 CE. They were most likely descendants of a second or third wave of settlers who displaced earlier nomadic hunter-gatherers. These earlier settlers were themselves descendants of peoples who had come across the Bering Sea land bridge to North America towards the end of the last great ice age. Another theory says they might have been the descendants of Pacific Islanders who sailed to the shores of North America.

The next incursion was of Spanish priests, soldiers, and settlers who colonized San Francisco in 1776, descendants of sixteenth century Spanish conquistadores from Mexico, Mexican aborigines, blacks, and those of mixed descent. While they settled along the eastern half of the San Francisco Peninsula, they seem to have ignored some of the northeast portion (where the Tenderloin would appear later), for it was one of the few places in the region that was never part of one of the Spanish or Mexican land grants awarded during that era.

The next wave of settlers was in the 1830s in the form of small groups of ship-borne traders and overland trappers from the United States. One of these, an Englishman named William A. Richardson, jumped ship, settled here, and was later awarded a plot of land near Yerba Buena Cove, becoming the founder of the village of that name (later renamed San Francisco). But it wasn't until after the American capture and subsequent purchase of California from Mexico in 1846 that the first known settler of any description put down roots in a little valley southwest of the village. He was Hanoverian immigrant Henry Gerke, who in 1847 built what was probably the area's first dwelling on what is now Mason Street, between Eddy and Ellis, on the lot now occupied by a Glide Church family housing project. By the early 1850s it was called St. Ann's Valley by real estate dealers and residents.

Saint Ann's Valley went through a couple of modest spurts of development, mainly by a few families from the merchant and professional classes who moved there to get away from the crime and fires of San Francisco around the times of the first and second

Committees of Vigilance in 1851 and 1856. But the Valley remained an underpopulated settlement, isolated from the rest of San Francisco by a line of dunes and hills that extended west from Market Street, which blocked roads or streets from connecting with it.

But this was about to change. In May of 1859, grading contractor David Hewes cut, filled, and leveled a road for a steam railway for the Market Street Railroad. It ran along Market Street from Third to Valencia and out to Sixteenth Street. The subsequent cutting and grading of the Valley's sand dune trails into streets connected them to San Francisco's street grid for the first time.

In the city, as was the case elsewhere, development followed the street railroads. In St. Ann's Valley, the grading of its nearby streets and blocks, along with the later grading of Market Street, was done so quickly that after 1866 the city directories stopped referring to the Valley as a location. Grading had obliterated the Valley as a geographic feature while subsequent development had incorporated the area into the rest of San Francisco.

It developed into a residential and small business neighborhood over the next decade-and-a-half, with rows of residences for business and professional-class families. At that time, the area bounded by Fern Hill (now Nob Hill) on the north, Dupont Street (now Grant Avenue) on the east, Market Street on the south, and Van Ness Avenue on the west was well known as one of the neighborhoods people moved to if they had the means. The streets were composed mostly of single-family residences, and the farther north or west one traveled from Market Street, the swankier they became.

Though it's hard to believe today, mansions dotted the neighborhood in the 1860s and 1870s and were occupied by people like Michael Castle, a wholesale grocer whose wife's attire at parties included a black velvet gown studded with diamonds and her hair sprinkled with diamond dust. Next door, built in 1872 on a 50-vara lot on the southwest corner of O'Farrell and Leavenworth streets, was the two-story, bay-windowed and mansard-roofed mansion of Robert J. Johnson, a millionaire metal broker and merchant whose wife Kate owned between thirty and fifty Angora and Persian cats.

Comstock Silver King John Mackay bought his San Francisco mansion on O'Farrell Street in 1874 where the Great American Music Hall stands today. James Flood, another Comstock Silver King, lived on Mason Street between Eddy and Ellis from 1868 through 1871 (now a Tenderloin Neighborhood Development Corporation housing project), next door to cattle millionaire William Dunphy. Flood subsequently moved to Ellis Street between Jones and Leavenworth from 1872 through 1880 (now the Lassen Apartments senior housing project). Stockbroker William Burling built his mansion on the southwest corner of Eddy and Hyde streets in 1872, now a row of art deco buildings originally constructed as film exchanges.

One of San Francisco's judges, a former alcalde named George Hyde, lived on Geary Street between Leavenworth and Hyde from 1864 through 1891 (now the Earl Court Apartments). Mayor Henry P. Coon lived on the next block. Wealthy gasfitter and plumber James K. Prior lived in a mansion on the southwest corner of Mason and Eddy streets from 1860 through 1884 (now the Tenderloin Neighborhood Development Corporation's Ambassador Hotel). People like militia general Champion I. Hutchinson were listed on Powell Street between Ellis and O'Farrell from 1867 through 1871 (now the Villa Florence Hotel). Sheriff Patrick White lived just a block south, at 8 Powell, from 1867 through 1869 (now the Flood Building), and on Turk between Leavenworth and Hyde from 1871 through 1878 (now Fort Knox Self Storage).

The politics of the neighborhood reflected its residents: families headed by conservative businessmen and professionals, civic leaders, and merchants. In the 1850s, St. Ann's Valley was a Whig/Republican island in a Democratic sea and remained reliably Republican up until the middle of the Great Depression. It was a neighborhood of churches and schools. An observer standing on Nob Hill could look down over the Tenderloin and count ten church steeples, several religious schools, and even a convent (the latter now the site of the Presentation Community senior housing building just across the street from Glide Church). There were also some of San Francisco's toniest private schools, like the ill-fated St. Mary's Hall on the southeast corner of Powell and Geary streets (later the Lincoln Building); St. Ignatius College on Market Street between Fourth and Fifth (now Bloomingdale's); and the Clarke Institute on the southeast corner of Mason and O'Farrell (now the Hotel Nikko).

Several decades before the Tenderloin got its moniker, the area extending a few blocks east and west of where the cable car turnaround at Powell and Market streets is today was called St. Ann's Valley. When the section of the map shown here was surveyed in February of 1852, this locale had just twenty-one structures. These were mostly homesteads built by middle-class families who were fleeing the high crime district that Gold Rush San Francisco had become. This early ripple of development began around the time that the 1851 Committee of Vigilance, of which several of the new Valley residents were members, cleared out the worst of the criminals who had been terrorizing the populace since 1849. The Valley streets were just trails that meandered around the little hamlet in greater or lesser conformity to the street grid. It was so isolated that to get there one had to hike or ride across sand dunes north from the Mission Toll Road or southwest from Sutter and Dupont streets (now Sutter Street and Grant Avenue). [*Author's collection*]

St. Ignatius Church and the Academy of St. Ignatius were built in 1855 on the south side of Market Street between Fourth and Fifth (now Bloomingdale's). [*St. Ignatius Parish, San Francisco*]

An early St. Ann's Valley enterprise was a plant nursery and hot house operated by a couple of French horticulturists on the northwest corner of Powell and Eddy streets, called St. Ann's Garden (now the Forever 21 store and the Lofts at One Powell). Other ventures were scattered about the Valley at different times during the 1850s, including several livestock yards, a couple of slaughterhouses, a candle factory, several starch manufacturers, and a maker of fur garments. [*San Francisco City Directory*]

DAVID HEWES

David Hewes came to San Francisco via Panama in 1850. He became a grading contractor and was one of the first to level a building lot in St. Ann's Valley, on the northeast corner of Stockton and O'Farrell streets (now the site of Macy's men's store) in 1853 for the owner, George Amerige. In 1860, Hewes' business was engaged to build a roadbed for the Market Street Railroad from Third and Market streets to Valencia out to Sixteenth Street. After completing the project his firm was hired to level city blocks and grade thoroughfares along both sides of Market Street, including much of what is now the Tenderloin. [*Eben Putnam*]

Henry Owens was a shipwright who built a home on the north side of Eddy street between Hyde and Larkin (now a PG&E substation) in 1854, just past the western tip of St. Ann's Valley, when it was still sparsely settled sand hills and was geographically cut off from the town. He operated a shipyard at Steamboat Point near Third and Townsend. He also built a yacht, the *Dart*, in his front yard in the 1850s, when the area still had dirt paths instead of streets, and somehow hauled it to the Mission Toll Road and down Third Street to his ways to be launched. [*Overland Monthly and Out West Magazine*]

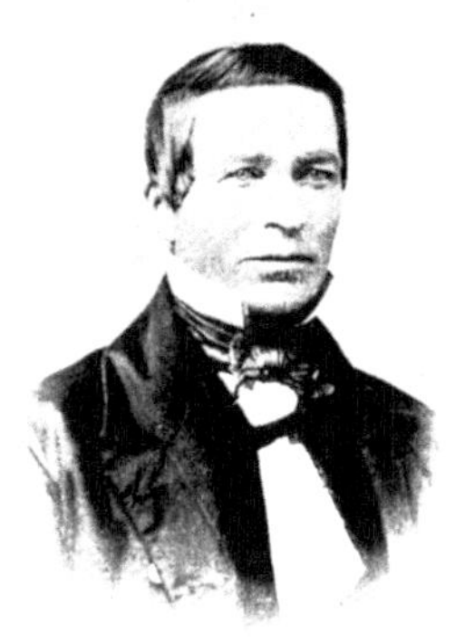

HENRY OWENS.

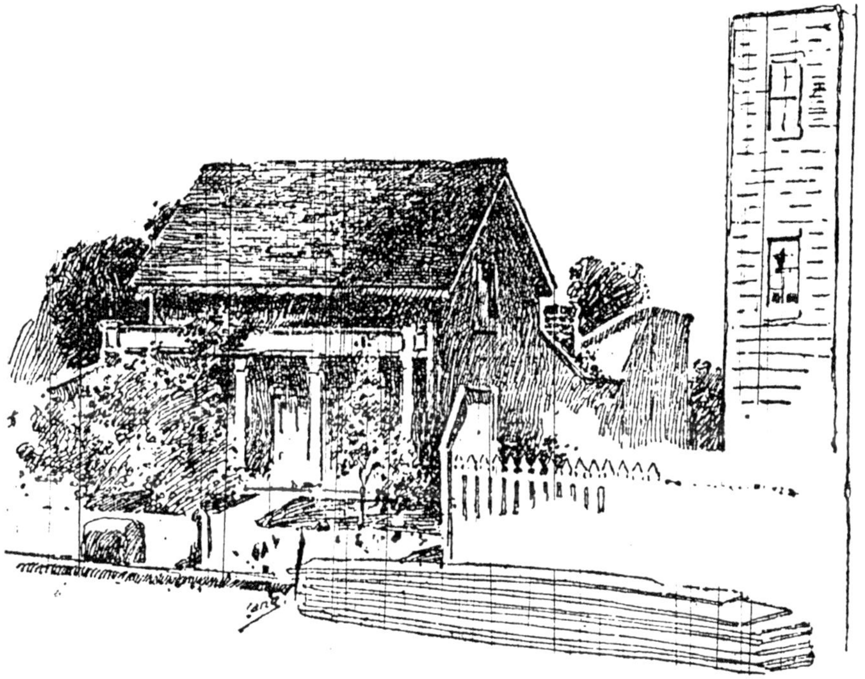

HISTORIC COTTAGE ON EDDY STREET, NEAR MARKET SOON TO PASS AWAY.
[*Sketched by a "Call" artist.*]

A more or less typical 1850s dwelling in St. Ann's Valley. Several newspaper articles reported it was built in either England or Boston and brought around Cape Horn to San Francisco in 1849 or 1850 as flat sections of floors, walls, ceilings, and roofing to be erected in what was then downtown or in St. Ann's Valley. By the late 1850s it was owned and occupied by the Williams family. According to census records and the city directories, somewhere between 1856 and 1858 this family, consisting of two English stonecutters, brothers named Francis and William, emigrated from New York with their mother and Francis' young daughter. They either built or bought the house and lived there while operating a marble cutting business in the large yard. [*San Francisco Call*]

Blacksmith and Forty-niner Jonathan Kittredge built or had shipped this Carpenter Gothic house in 1855 on the north side of Ellis Street between Powell and Mason (now the Hotel Fusion) years before the street was graded and sidewalks built. The house had twelve rooms, two stories, an attic, a small backyard orchard, an artesian well, a barn, and a cow. He lived there until his death in 1883. The photograph is dated 1865. [*California State Library*]

Kittredge was the youngest of fourteen children in a family from a small town in Massachusetts. His father died when he was just eight, and he was raised by an older brother who was a Presbyterian minister. He came around Cape Horn to San Francisco in 1849 with a load of miner's tools he manufactured himself. After going to the placer mines and catching "Panama fever," he opened a smithy in San Francisco and did well enough to buy property and build his house. He was hired to manage the iron works that he later purchased, lived the life of a successful businessman, and was active in Republican politics. [*San Francisco Call*]

At age eighteen, John Sullivan, his two younger brothers, and his younger sister were orphaned in Missouri and his younger sister were orphaned in Missouri in 1844 when their parents died while while the family was preparing to emigrate to California. Despite this, he brought his siblings across the plains and mountains to the village of Yerba Buena as part of the Murphy-Stephens party, the third overland expedition and first wagon train to reach California. Eleven years later, when he was listed in the 1856 city directory as residing in St. Ann's Valley on Ellis Street between Stockton and Powell, he had already made a small fortune in the placer mines and from selling supplies to the miners, and was reaping profits from sales of early grants and purchases of San Francisco real estate. He was one of early land grants and purchases of San Francisco real estate. His daughter married James Phelan and their descendants were long involved in San Francisco's development and history. [*Presentation Archives, San Francisco*]

Ludovic Galley was the San Francisco representative of the Parisian firm of Lecacheux, Galley, & Co. He was listed in the city directories on the southwest corner of Turk and Taylor streets (now the Grand Apartments) from 1856 through 1858, when he learned his wife was coming from France to visit him. He packed his live-in mistress back to France, but she only got as far as Mazatlan when she realized she was pregnant. She returned to San Francisco, expecting his support, but he spurned her. She then stabbed Ludovic, which he barely survived. Declining to press charges, he hid to avoid a subpoena to testify in her trial. She was ultimately discharged from jail for lack of evidence and gave birth to their daughter. Meanwhile, Galley's wife arrived, learned about the affair, and as soon as they could they left for France. But Galley died from his wound while they were passing through Acapulco. Madame Galley brought his body to Le Havre where she had it interred. She attended Mass the next morning, traveled outside the city, and committed suicide by shooting herself under a tree. [*San Francisco City Directory*]

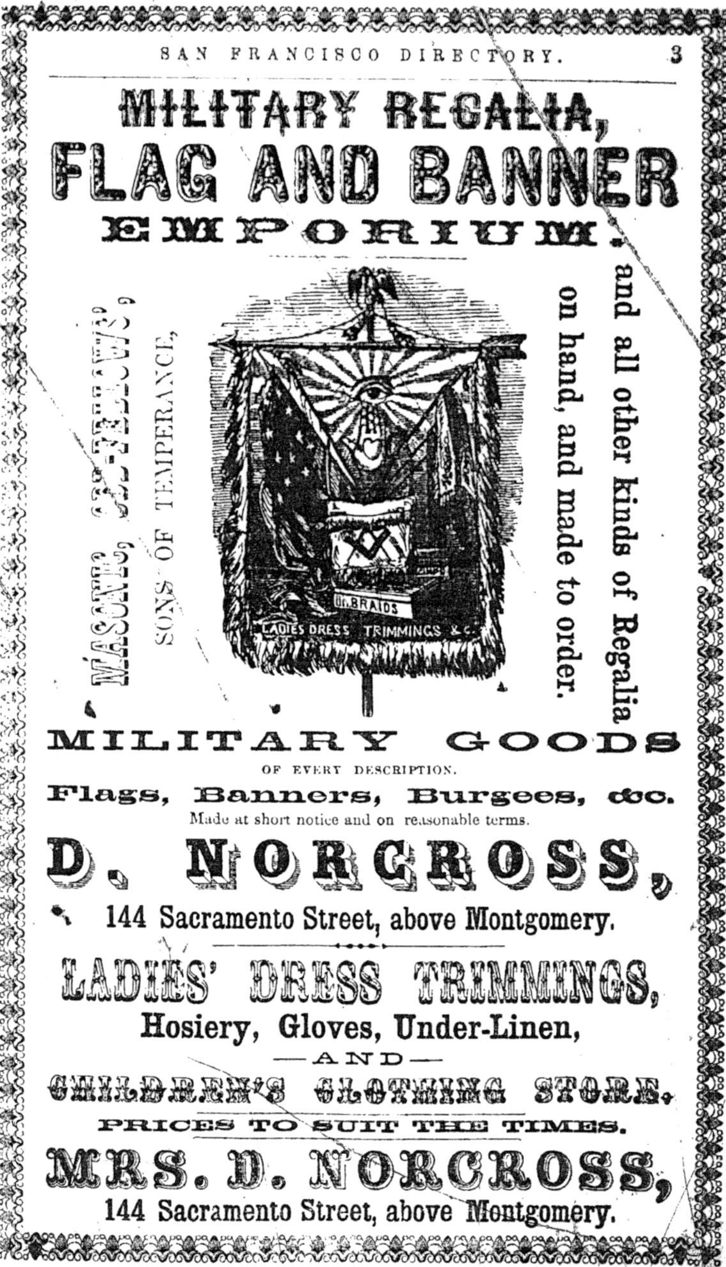

A manufacturer and retailer of military uniforms and lodge regalia, Daniel Norcross left Philadelphia to sail to San Francisco in 1849, where, instead of going to the placer mines, he opened his business. Norcross and his wife, Harriet, were first listed as residing on the northern edge of St. Ann's Valley in 1856 on the south side of O'Farrell Street between Taylor and Jones (now the Winton Hotel). The Norcrosses were remarkable for their time and place because Harriet, a respectable, middle-class, married woman with children, ran her own business selling decorative trimmings for dresses, as well as lingerie and children's clothing. Even more unusual, she advertised the business under her own name. (*San Francisco City Directory*)

Sargent Shaw Morton Is Summoned

Passes Away at His Alameda Home

Was Formerly Well Known Business Man and a Supervisor in This City

ALAMEDA, February 6.—Sargent Shaw Morton, one of San Francisco's earliest settlers and for years prominent in political circles in that city, died last night at his home, 1236 Park street, this city. Following his retirement from business, Morton had resided in Alameda fifteen years.

Morton was born in Standish, Me., eighty-three years ago. He came to San Francisco in 1850 by way of Panama. He established a drayage business, which he later conducted with his brothers, John and Reuben Morton, as the Morton Drayage Company.

Morton was a Supervisor in San Francisco in the late eighties and later became Receiver of the United States Land Office there. His brother, Reuben Morton, was for years president of the California-street Railway Company in San Francisco. Deceased, up to his death, took an interest in county, State and national affairs.

Morton is survived by a daughter, Mrs. Jesse Rogers of Alameda, and a son, Frank Morton of San Francisco.

CANADIAN POLICE
ARREST SUSPECT

SARGENT S. MORTON

Sargent Morton came to San Francisco from Maine via Panama in 1850 and was followed later by two of his brothers, John and Reuben. They started a drayage business that became one of the largest in San Francisco. Their first listed address was in 1856 on the edge of St. Ann's Valley around Ellis and O'Farrell streets between Mason and Taylor (now the Hilton Hotel). They built a large yard and barn on this block for their business as well as a large house and a dormitory building for around twenty of their workers, who were mostly Irish teamsters. [*San Francisco Chronicle*]

In 1856, Irish immigrant and sail maker Thomas W. McColliam was listed on the north side of Eddy Street, between Taylor and Jones (now Boeddeker Park). In the mid 1860s he began buying ships and established a cod fishery south of the Aleutian Islands. According to architectural historian William Kostura, the double fronted Italianate on the left in this photograph was built for the McColliams in 1870, apparently replacing their earlier home on this site. [*Western Neighborhoods Project/Private collector*]

Andrew Louderback was eighteen when he came to San Francisco from Philadelphia with his parents and younger brother by ship through the Straits of Magellan in 1849. After working in the placer mines, he returned to San Francisco and became a successful fish and game dealer, donating 150 pounds of game to the Catholic, Protestant, and Hebrew orphanges every Christmas. He bought a 50-vara lot on the northwest corner of Eddy and Leavenworth streets (now the Cadillac Hotel) where he built two sets of row houses, occupying several of them over the following years. A Republican activist, he was once nearly arrested on a charge of attempting to suborn a grand juror. [*San Francisco Call*]

This photograph of St. Ann's Valley is dated 1858. The area's development was somewhat denser than seen in the image because many buildings are hidden behind the sand dunes. The road running horizontally across the middle of the picture is the Mission Toll Road. The parallel line below it towards the right is the future route of Market Street. The dark building in the center of the photograph is the home of John Sullivan, located on the north side of Ellis between Stockton and Powell (now a parking lot). The buildings just to the left are St. Ignatius Church and the Academy of St. Ignatius, built on the south side of Market Street between Fourth and Fifth (now Bloomingdale's) in 1855. The building just to the right of Sullivan's house is the two-story home of Nathaniel Lane on the southwest corner of Powell and Ellis streets. In front of the Lane house is the home of the Morton brothers on O'Farrell and Taylor streets (now the Hilton Hotel), owners of one of San Francisco's largest drayage companies. Just in front of the Mortons is the dormitory where about twenty of their teamsters roomed. Barely visible behind the left and right sides of the Morton residence is the home of Henry Gerke with the fence surrounding his large lot on the north side of Mason Street, between Eddy and Ellis (now a Glide Church family housing project). According to one source, Gerke built there around 1847, likely making him the first settler in St. Ann's Valley. [*Bancroft Library*]

The Market Street Railroad opened on July 4, 1860 and was much used at first. Later competition from horse car lines on adjacent streets that ran without smoke on smoother tracks with fewer derailments forced the Market Street Railroad to switch from steam to horse power in the late 1860s. A steam dummy (a small steam engine disguised as a horse car in the hope that it wouldn't frighten the horses with which it shared the streets) pulled the passenger cars. It was much more expensive to operate than a horse car, but was necessary because some of the grades on Market Street were still too steep for horse power. But by the mid-1860s Market Street had been regraded to a shallower slope, allowing the company to change over to the slower but gentler and cheaper horse cars. The photograph is dated 1864 and shows the corner of Market and Kearny streets looking southwest along Market Street towards a car in the distance being pulled by a steam dummy. The cars had an open upper deck with benches that faced the sidewalks. [*San Francisco History Center/San Francisco Public Library*]

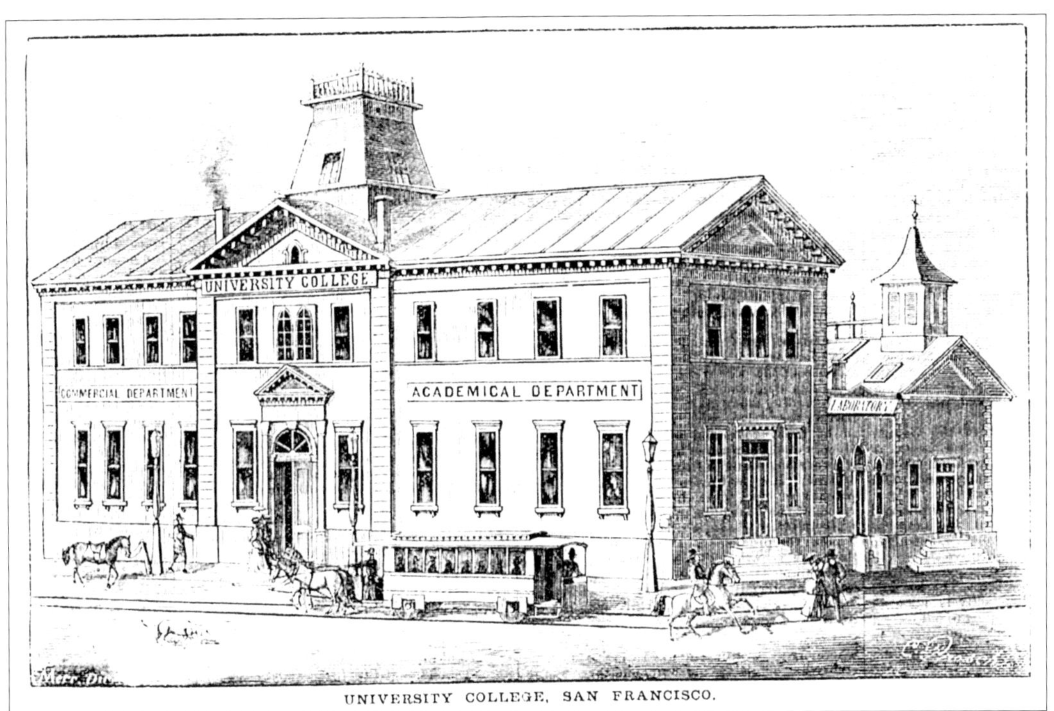

UNIVERSITY COLLEGE, SAN FRANCISCO.

City College of San Francisco started out as a Presbyterian school in the basement of Calvary Church when it was still on lower Bush Street before the congregation moved to the northwest corner of Powell and Geary streets (now the St. Francis Hotel). In early 1861, construction of the school's first building was completed on the southeast corner of Geary and Stockton streets (now Neiman Marcus) to make room in the old church's basement for a girls school. City College provided what was for the time a typical college prep education. Offerings included courses on mining and evaluating precious metals that grew into a School of Mining. The buildings were moved to Haight Street above Octavia in 1876. [*Pacific Rural Press*]

Marcus D. Boruck lived at several locations on the affluent northern edges of St. Ann's Valley from 1863 through 1880, after which he moved to Pacific Heights. He was a leader in the Republican politics of the Eighth Ward, which encompassed most of the future Tenderloin. He was prominent in the state Republican Party and in the state legislature where he was chief clerk over several sessions of both the assembly and the senate. He published two monthly journals: the *Spirit of the Times* was popularly called the "horse paper" because of his long interest in racing, while the *Fireman's Journal* advocated for the San Francisco volunteer fire companies, Boruck being a member of the California Engine Comapny No. 4. It also supported the Exempt Firemen, a fraternal society of former volunteer firemen. Boruck was a complex individual. He initiated and led efforts to recruit blacks into the Republican Party. He once backed down a crowd of "the gods,"—rabble rousers in a theater in the cheap upper tier—when they demanded the expulsion of a Chinese diplomat who was a guest of white friends in one of the boxes. On the other hand, he left the Republicans for a time to join the American Party, composed mainly of disenchanted Republican nativist "Know Nothings." This defection prompted the acerbic Ambrose Bierce to publish a scurrilously scathing denunciation of Boruck in a poem titled *The American Party*. He fearlessly exposed political corruption when and where he found it, yet he was an unapologetic supporter of the Central Pacific Railroad. Despite his numerous political, social, and business connections, he was never rich or well off. Even his political enemies respected him for his integrity, his competence, and his hard work. And, he was the first chief clerk in the state legislature to hire women as assistant clerks for their greater efficiency and honesty. [*Gayle Marin*]

The three-story Italianate Victorian in the foreground of this photograph (dated 1890) was the home of cattle baron William Dunphy and his family on Mason Street between Eddy and Ellis from 1864 through 1886. The United Presbyterian Church was next door, built in 1870 on the lot formerly occupied by Henry Gerke, the Valley's first settler. Both sites are now a Glide family housing project. [*Western Neighborhoods Project/Private collector*]

The City Female Seminary moved to the southeast corner of O'Farrell and Mason streets (shown here) in early 1864, and was renamed the Clarke Institute in 1872 after the death of its founder, Rev. Charles Russell Clarke. It was kept going by his wife Charlotte, who was also a successful neighborhood real estate investor and manager, until 1883. The school graduated a number of well known San Franciscans, including author Gertrude Atherton. At some point it apparently admitted boys. [*San Francisco History Center/San Francisco Public Library*]

This double-fronted Victorian on the north side of Geary Street between Leavenworth and Hyde was typical of the kinds of houses built along Geary Street between Stockton and Van Ness in the 1860s and 1870s. Benjamin F. Peixotto lived in the building in the far left (now the Geary Manor and Annex Apartments) in 1870 and 1871. He was a successful Jewish dry goods merchant and attorney just before he was appointed consul to the violently antisemitic country of Romania in an attempt by the administration of Ulysses S. Grant to aid the Romanian Jews. [*Society of California Pioneers*]

By the early 1860s, St. Ignatius Church's congregation and the Academy of St. Ignatius' student body had grown to the point where they needed larger quarters. This brick edifice was completed on the school's 100-vara lot in 1865. The school was renamed St. Ignatius College when it received a state charter that year. It remained in this location until 1883, when it was moved to a new building on Van Ness Avenue and Hayes Street. [*San Francisco History Center/San Francisco Public Library*]

This is the intersection of Market, Powell, and Eddy streets in 1866. In the late 1850s there were several fires in the Valley, none of which could be extinguished because there were no streets to connect the the little community to the volunteer fire companies in town. In 1859 the residents formed their own company, naming it The Independent, and purchased a "Red Crab" engine from New York, garaging it in one of these buildings. [*San Francisco History Center/San Francisco Public Library*]

Market Street between Powell and Mason in 1866. A new double railroad track is being laid along Market Street for the conversion from steam to horse cars. Walter Rice and Emiliano Echeverria wrote in *When Steam Ran on the Streets of San Francisco* that by this time the Market Street Railroad had extended its line from Sixteenth and Valencia, near The Willows, to the Twenty-Fifth Street and Valencia depot of the San Francisco & San Jose Railroad. [*San Francisco History Center/San Francisco Public Library*]

This incorrectly dated photograph of Turk Street between Market and Taylor was actually taken in 1866. The Market Street grade was still inclined, climbing above Turk Street, leaving a declivity that was the last geographic remnant of St. Ann's Valley. That part of the neighborhood had drainage and flooding problems for years until the slope on this part of Market Street was finally levelled and a storm drainage system installed. Note the almost exclusively residential character of this area. [*Author's collection*]

This 1867 photograph shows the south side of Geary Street between Stockton and Powell (now Macy's), directly across from Union Square. The entire neighborhood looked like this— respectably residential, with many single family homes. The church in the middle of the block was the first St. Mark's Church, built in 1863, known at that time as the United German Evangelical Lutheran Congregation of St. Mark's Church. The streetcar tracks turning west from Stockton Street onto Geary were for the Central Railroad, which started carrying passengers through St. Ann's Valley in 1863. [*San Francisco History Center, San Francisco Public Library*]

In 1868 the cornerstone was laid for the construction of the Sacred Heart Presentation Convent on the southwest corner of Ellis and Taylor streets (now the Presentation Community senior housing project). The sisters operated a Catholic School there until the 1906 earthquake and fire destroyed it. The school was one of the centers of a legislative controversy in the 1870s over whether or not the state should fund religious schools. In the end, the doctrine of the separation of church and state prevailed. The photograph is dated 1890. [*Presentation Archives, San Francisco*]

Alexander P. Crittenden was a lawyer from the patrician South who started an affair with Laura D. Fair, the proprietress of the Virginia City boarding house where he and his wife and family were staying in the 1860s. The family and Mrs. Fair moved separately to San Francisco, where Crittenden's wife finally learned of the affair and subsequently took herself and the children back east with her. Crittenden moved into lodgings on the south side of Ellis Street between Powell and Mason (now the Hilton Parc 55 Hotel) around 1867 or 1868 and continued to see Mrs. Fair. In 1870, he reconciled with his wife and family and they returned to San Francisco to rejoin him. He went to Oakland to meet their train, and on the ferry back to San Francisco, Mrs. Fair, who had followed him, shot and killed Crittenden when she saw them together. The widow and her children moved into Crittenden's rooms. They later moved several blocks west on the south side of Ellis Street between Leavenworth and Hyde (now the 555 Ellis Apartments, a subsidized housing project for homeless families). Several years later the family moved again to the southeast corner of Taylor and Eddy (now the Moderne Hotel and PianoFight). Mrs. Fair was tried twice for the killing and was finally acquitted. [*Clements Library, University of Michigan, Ann Arbor*]

As the Central Presbyterian Church's congregation grew, it moved three blocks west from Mission Street to Tyler Street (now Golden Gate Avenue) between Taylor and Jones into a new building in 1869. But it outgrew the new church in just three years, which was replaced with the much larger Central Presbyterian Tabernacle shown here. The design was octagonal, with the pews arranged in semicircles on risers like in a theater, gazing down upon the pulpit. This showed the congregation was in keeping with the popular architectural theories of Orson Squire Fowler, "America's foremost lecturer and writer on phrenology" as put forth in his widely read book, *The Octagon House: A Home for All, or a New, Cheap, Convenient, and Superior Mode of Building*, published in 1848. As the congregants continued to move farther west, the church moved again in 1883, this time four blocks west to the northeast corner of Golden Gate Avenue and Polk Street (now the Federal Building). [*San Francisco History Center/San Francisco Public Library*]

The Club Stables was opened about 1869 by Daniel C. McGlynn on the west side of Taylor Street between O'Farrell and Geary (now a parking garage). By 1879, it belonged to Charles S. Crittenden, who ran it as one of his livery, boarding, and sale stables through 1888. It was owned next by Richard D. Ledgett from 1889 through 1894, who once allowed a duel to be staged in the building. It was run as a stable until the 1906 earthquake and fire and rebuilt as a garage in 1912. [*Glenn Koch Collection*]

The German Roman Catholic congregation of St. Boniface church bought the middle 50-vara lot on the south side of Tyler Street (now Golden Gate Avenue) between Jones and Leavenworth and built a new church and priest's residence in 1870 when they moved from downtown. In 1887 they built a larger church (shown here) to accommodate their growing flock. [*Franciscan Friars, Saint Barbara Province*]

Bonanza King John Mackay and his wife Marie, the latter wearing a costly six-string pearl choker. According to Oscar Lewis in his book *Silver Kings*, Mackay was a shrewd but uneducated and unpretentious Irishman who spent most of his time in Virginia City managing their forty-percent share of the Mackay-Fair-Flood-O'Brien mining holdings. However, Mrs. Mackay was socially ambitious and her first step was to buy a small mansion in San Francisco in 1874 on the south side of O'Farrell Street between Larkin and Polk (now the Great American Music Hall). She entertained frequently and was socially prominent, but came to feel San Francisco was a social backwater, and in 1876 they sold the house to their business manager, Cornelius O'Connor, and moved to New York. [*San Francisco Chronicle/Author's collection*]

The Christian Brothers built Sacred Heart College, a Catholic School for boys, on the southeast corner of Eddy and Larkin streets in 1874 (now the site of Saigon Sandwich and HTL 587), where it was an immediate success. It had a number of illustrious alumni, among them Gentleman Jim Corbett who took the world heavyweight boxing title from John L. Sullivan in 1892. Corbett came to Sacred Heart after he was expelled from St. Ignatius College for an after hours fight in back of the school. He was then expelled from Sacred Heart after he ran away from a teacher who was going to hit his hands with a ruler for some minor infraction. [*Western Narighborhoods Project/Private collector*]

Turnvereins were German gymnastic and patriotic associations, a legacy of the early nineteenth century German nationalist Friedrich Ludwig Jahn. In 1866, the San Francisco Turn Verein built a hall on the north side of O'Farrell Street between Mason and Taylor (now the Downtown Center Garage) which they occupied for about a decade. They then sold it to the Swedenborgian Church (known in those days as the Free-Thinking German Church) and built a new and larger hall (shown here) on the south side of Turk Street between Leavenworth and Hyde in 1875 (later site of the YMCA Hotel, and now the Oasis Apartments). [*San Francisco History Center/San Francisco Public Library*]

Robert C. Johnson was a hard-as-nails businessman who inherited several million dollars from his father and married the educated, cultured, charitable, and gracious Kate Birdsall. In 1873, they built a two-story mansion with a mansard roof and a garden on the 50-vara lot on the southwest corner of O'Farrell and Leavenworth streets (now the Farrellworth Apartments) and filled it with art. [*Presentation Archives, San Francisco*]

In 1875, she bought artist Toby Rosenthal's painting *Elaine* after the man who commissioned the work, another San Franciscan named Tiburcio Parrott, failed to pay for it. [*Author's collection*]

Mrs. Johnson allowed the art dealer to exhibit *Elaine* at Snow's Gallery on the corner of Kearny and Morton streets. The canvas was stolen on the third night of the exhibition by a gang, two of whom are shown here: Thomas J. Wallace and William "Cut Face" Donohue. The next day Mrs. Johnson's customary graciousness wasn't in evidence when she gave her opinion of the then unknown thief: "He should either be hanged, drawn and quartered, or broken on the wheel … But since these antique methods of punishment cannot be revived, I would have him scourged at the whipping post."[1] Meanwhile, the newspapers went into ecstasies of reportage and speculation and there was a line of people extending down the block waiting to get into Snow's gallery to see the frame that the painting had been cut out of. Despite the drama, the police arrested the culprits in just two days and recovered the painting the next day. [*Bancroft Library*]

After her husband died in 1899, Mrs. Johnson commissioned Austrian painter Carl Kahler, who was living in San Francisco, to paint a portrait of her forty-two Angora and Persian cats. Kahler, who had never before painted a cat, spent two years drawing them and completed a 6 by 8 foot, 227-pound painting of the felines, titled *My Wife's Lovers*. After Mrs. Johnson died, the cats were left in the care of a distant relative in North Beach along with $20,000 to care for them. [*Author's collection*]

Opposite: Harriet Lane Levy grew up at 920 O'Farrell Street between Polk and Van Ness (now the AMC Theater). Unusual for the time, she graduated from Cal Berkeley and pursued a career as a writer. She was a close friend of the housekeeper of the Levison family next door, a woman named Alice who was the orphaned granddaughter of the family patriarch. Both women yearned for an artistic and literary life instead of their dull middle-class Jewish family existences. In 1907 they were invited by Harriet's friends Michael and Sarah Stein to visit the Steins in Paris where they were introduced to Michael's brother and sister, Leo and Gertrude Stein. Over the following weeks and months Gertrude fell in love with Alice, who of course was Alice Babette Toklas, and wooed her away from Harriet. [*Bancroft Library*]

According to the June 21, 1875 *San Francisco Chronicle*, the First Baptist Church's plan to move from its original location on Washington Street near Stockton was because of the property's depreciation in value as Chinatown moved closer to it, resulting in, according to them, crowds of heathens on the sidewalks. They built a new church (shown here) on the north side of Eddy Street between Jones and Leavenworth (now the Indochinese Community Development Corporation's Nathan Building) and celebrated its first service in January of 1876. A novel feature of the new structure was that the floor supporting the dais and pulpit could be mechanically rolled back to reveal the heated baptismal pool beneath it. Candidates who wanted to be baptized walked down a set of steps on either side of the main hall to enter the water. [*San Francisco Chronicle*]

Dancer Isadora Duncan, or Angela Dora as she was named by her parents, was born in a double fronted house on the northwest corner of Geary and Taylor streets (now the Geary-Taylor Apartments) in May 1877. After her parents divorced, Angela, her mother, and her siblings moved across the Bay to Oakland where they lived in genteel poverty while the former Mrs. Duncan taught her children to appreciate the arts. In her autobiography Duncan attributed the development of her spontaneous dance style, as well as her lifestyle, to the lack of parental supervision occasioned by her mother being out during the days and evenings to give music lessons to support the family. [*Author's collection*]

In the 1870s, the southwest corner of Geary and Leavenworth streets (shown here) was the location of the Yee Wah wash house, one of six or more Chinese laundries in the neighborhood. On June 23, 1877, a mob of around 200 men broke away from an anti-Chinese demonstration in front of the new City Hall across from McAllister and Leavenworth streets. They went up Leavenworth Street and wrecked Charley's wash house on Tyler Street (now Golden Gate Avenue). Two police officers were injured when stones were thrown at them while they tried to protect the building. The mob then wrecked the Sin Shing wash house on Turk Street. When a Chinese man from the laundry ran into a grocery next door, some of the rioters broke its display windows and stole bottles of whiskey which they passed amongst themselves. The mob then resumed their march up Leavenworth Street to Geary, where the men wrecked the Yee Wah wash house and set it ablaze, destroying several other shops and the apartments above it. The occupants managed to escape but when the fire department arrived and tried to extiguish the blaze, members of the mob cut the hoses. However, many other wash houses escaped notice by removing their signs to present an anonymous appearance and closing up shop. This was the beginning of three days and nights of anti-Chinese riots in San Francisco that led to the formation of the citizen's axe handle brigade led by businessman William Coleman. Directed by officials, the brigade assisted the police during the riots. [*Author's collection*]

Endnotes

1. Robert O'Brien, *This is San Francisco* (San Francisco, Chronicle Books, 1948), 90.

TWO

THE RISE OF THE TENDERLOIN

In San Francisco, people tend to think of the Tenderloin's problems as a unique set of social issues that started in the 1960s. But these problems really began well over a hundred years ago in much the same manner that other residential districts in other urban areas around the globe evolved into inner cities throughout the industrial age. In San Francisco, it started in the 1870s with the southwestern movement of the hotel and theater districts from what was then an aging downtown section.

In 1872, small hotels began appearing along Turk Street and other nearby thoroughfares north and west of Market Street. In 1876, the area's first theater, Baldwin's Academy of Music, opened inside the massive Baldwin Hotel on the corner of Market and Powell streets (now the Flood Building). (Since the hotel wasn't completed for another year, patrons had the unique experience of seeing a play in a theater inside a building that was still under construction.) Just across the street at Powell and Eddy, where the old Bank of America building is now, the St. Ann's Building was erected in 1877, the neighborhood's first office block. In 1879, the Tivoli Gardens moved from Sutter and Stockton streets to Eddy between Powell and Mason and soon changed its entertainment format from *Biergarten* music and refreshments to light opera.

These three developments, the hotels, the theaters, and an office block, began the transformation of this middle- and upper-class residential district into San Francisco's new hotel, entertainment, and upscale vice district. Residents who saw the beginnings of these trends moved farther west into the emerging Western Addition and Pacific Heights neighborhoods, or in some cases to estates or growing towns on the San Francisco Peninsula. What had been mansions became fancy hotels and lodging houses, and what had been single family residences were subdivided into flats or became rooming houses. In 1884, the area's first upscale brothel, called a parlor house in the period's patois, opened on Ellis Street between Mason and Taylor, just half a block east of the Sacred Heart Presentation Convent and girls' school. By the 1890s, the east half of the neighborhood had many hotels and rooming houses, half a dozen theaters, a growing number of restaurants, and at least a dozen parlor houses of greater or lesser repute. It was also where people who worked in the neighborhood lived, in the area's hotels, rooming houses, apartments, and remaining homes.

Yet a number of early residents stuck it out, and the neighborhood west of Jones Street stayed largely middle- and upper-class residential, especially in the northwest quadrant, up until 1906. Meanwhile, the area east of Jones Street had become the Tenderloin.

No one knows exactly how the Tenderloin got its name, though there are quite a few urban legends. But, like so many other things in nineteenth-century California, the most famous one came from back east. A police officer named Captain Alexander "Clubber" Williams, so-called because of his fame as a nightstick artist, was assigned to New York City's Satan's Circus neighborhood in 1876 in what is now Chelsea and part of Midtown Manhattan, which was then New York's silk-stocking hotel, entertainment, and vice district. This assignment was destined to make him rich because of the protection money he would extort from the upscale vice venues in the neighborhood. As one version of the story goes, a newspaper reporter ran into Williams entering Delmonico's restaurant (an eatery which an honest police captain would not have been able to afford) and asked him how he liked his new assignment. He is alleged to have replied, "I have had chuck for a long time, and now I'm going to eat tenderloin."[1] According to the legend, the name stuck and became the district's new appellation.

To this day, no one's been able to track any of these stories to their sources. But in 1887, just a decade later, the following appeared in the New York *Evening World*: "In the 'tenderloin' districts Nicoli is receiving an immense vote,"[2] making it the first newspaper to use the word *tenderloin* to refer to a geographic area instead of a cut of meat. In 1888, the *San Francisco Chronicle* reprinted an article from the *New York Sun*, which included the phrase "One of the curiosities of the big 'Tenderloin' precinct,"[3] referring to Satan's Circus. By 1891, the word was being used in newspapers across the country (this being the age of the telegraph) to refer to their vice districts, and this included California towns and cities such as Los Angeles, Santa Cruz, Redding, and San Francisco. But it wasn't until the fall of 1893 that newspapers started naming the area south of Union Square and west of Dupont Street as *the* Tenderloin.

The Tenderloin before the 1906 earthquake and fire was very much as described in the Introduction. It became a center for organizing and gambling on horse races, boxing matches, and various other sports. Places like Harry Corbett's saloon and betting parlor, on Ellis Street between Stockton and Powell, were famous as locations to get the most accurate odds or to see a favorite pugilist.

The Tenderloin was also the terminus of the cocktail route, an institution that San Francisco historian Gary Kamiya wrote:

> started on Montgomery Street around Washington, headed unsteadily south six blocks
> to Sutter, stumbled over a block to Kearny, staggered up to Powell and passed out around
> Eddy and Mason. Along the way, the Cocktail Route passed no fewer than 20 saloons,
> which included the most famous and well appointed drinking establishments in the city.
> All of them served, in addition to the potent beverages that gave the route its name, a
> mouthwateringly munificent free lunch. The Route's all-male ranks of regulars included
> respectable businessmen and politicians, as well as a miscellaneous crew of drink cadgers,

skirt chasers and opportunistic gourmands known as 'free lunch fiends.' They followed
an unvarying routine. Around 5 p.m., these gentlemen would close down their offices,
don their Prince Albert frock coats and hats, and stroll into the street, lighting up their
stogies. Ten blocks and as many as 20 Champagne cocktails, Bonanzas or Pisco punches
later, they would finish up and be delivered to their Nob Hill homes, to be greeted by the
icy stares of their wives.[4]

The Tenderloin was where many of the city's fraternal organizations had their lodge
headquarters with their weekly and monthly meetings. This accounted for the amazing
number of newspaper advertisements for purloined diamond stick pins with lodge
devices by gentlemen who would hit the Tenderloin saloons after a lodge affair.

As the center of the new theater district the Tenderloin offered three flavors. There
was legitimate theater like the Alcazar and the Tivoli Opera; there were vaudeville and
variety at places like the Orpheum and the Wigwam; and there were dives called "concert
saloons" where the waitresses doubled as stage performers, when they weren't cadging
drinks from customers. Finally, there were beer halls of greater or lesser respectability,
where families and singles came to quaff, snack on foods like German sausages, and
listen to some of the well-known *Bierhalle* music of the day, such as Herr Stark and his
Vienna Orchestra.

The Tenderloin also became a center for San Francisco's emerging labor unions. In
the 1890s and up until 1906, more and more unions headquartered in the Tenderloin,
particularly those representing restaurant and hotel workers and musicians, but also
building trades workers and others. On any night of the week it was an odds-on bet
that there was a union meeting being held somewhere in the neighborhood, and much
of the labor unrest in San Francisco during that period was planned in various union
meeting rooms in the Tenderloin.

The nonprofit service agencies in the Tenderloin today were by no means the first
in the neighborhood. There were a variety of charitable institutions, especially before
the 1906 earthquake and fire. The Eureka Benevolent Society, which gave aid to needy
German Jews, rented several different locations in the Tenderloin before it built its own
structure in 1900 on O'Farrell Street between Taylor and Jones. There were two free
medical clinics for the destitute, one on the City College Campus at Geary and Stockton
streets, and another on Ellis Street between Jones and Leavenworth. There was a home
for homeless boys on Powell Street.

When the Cliff House was built at Lands End, when the Half Mile race track was laid
out at Geary and Twenty-Fifth Avenue in the 1860s, and when Golden Gate Park and
the Bay District Track at Geary and Fifth Avenue were developed in the 1870s, many
of the city's livery stables began locating in the Tenderloin because of its proximity to
Bush and Geary streets and to Golden Gate Avenue, which in those days were the main
routes to those attractions. On weekends it was fashionable for young men to rent a rig
and drive their ladies out to the park and back, or for a group of young bucks to drive
out to the Cliff House or one of the tracks during racing season.

Beginning in early 1905, San Francisco's first automobile dealerships opened along Golden Gate Avenue in the west half of the neighborhood on the assumption that those who could afford to own or rent horses and rigs for pleasure trips were a natural market for automobiles; and so, the dealerships located their showrooms where they would be seen by these potential customers as they drove by. This grew into San Francisco's first Auto Row after the 1906 earthquake and fire. This was partly because Golden Gate Avenue was for some time almost the only open route from Market Street to the undamaged west half of the city. Even when the development of the new Civic Center in 1912 forced many of the dealerships to relocate along Van Ness Avenue, others stayed on those blocks of Golden Gate not affected by the construction.

Despite this, the west half of the neighborhood remained a largely residential family district, especially before the 1906 earthquake and fire and after the 1915 Pacific Panama International Exhibition when it developed into an apartment district that stretched from the Tenderloin up into Lower Nob Hill. The neighborhood's churches and schools (there were many of these up until the 1906 earthquake and fire, including three public grammar schools) represented an aspect of Tenderloin life mostly ignored by historians, overshadowed as it was by the more notorious events in the eastern half of the district. It wasn't that it was unusual to have children in a neighborhood like the Tenderloin, it was that the children had been there all along, even when the rise of the Tenderloin started pushing families into the western half of the district. After the earthquake and fire, the public grammar school on Eddy Street between Polk and Van Ness was rebuilt and continued to educate returning Tenderloin (and other) children until it closed in 1944.

While the west half of the district stayed relatively peaceful, the east half was increasingly known for its crime, especially in the area's southeast quadrant. In particular, street crime was a growing problem. During this period, there arose a protection racket that grew so large it shielded vice and crime from the legal system throughout San Francisco. There was a period in which the racket had so many police and court employees on the take that its lawyers would frequently arrive at the police station to bail out the client before the arresting officer had even arrived with the prisoner.

The delineation of the neighborhood into east and west halves brings up an often-asked question: where exactly was the Tenderloin? The answer depended on the decade being asked about. But in general, the Tenderloin was considered by most San Franciscans to start at around Dupont Street (now Grant Avenue), at first extending west to around Taylor, and later another block west to Jones, and extending south from Geary to Market Street until the 1906 earthquake and fire. After this it shifted west to Stockton and extended all the way to Larkin Street, still encompassing Geary Street south to Market. After World War II it shifted farther west to Polk Street and even Van Ness Avenue while development around Union Square pushed its eastern boundary to Powell Street in the 1960s. Sometime after the 1960s, the northern boundary moved from Geary Street up to Post. By the 1990s, massive new hotel projects and conversions of residential hotels into tourist hotels moved the eastern boundary another block west to Mason Street.

Meanwhile, the Tenderloin kept its name until the 1906 disaster caused the entire entertainment and vice district to flee to the Fillmore Street shopping district between Turk and Geary streets, which in those days was still called the Western Addition and was considered part of uptown San Francisco. This was a strictly residential and small merchant section that had little experience with vice and entertainment. When the press began referring to the neighborhood as the Uptown Tenderloin, Western Addition residents and businesses reacted predictably. In a relatively short time the brothels and gamblers found themselves expelled from the area. This created another wave of citizen protest when they tried to set up shop in other residential neighborhoods. The situation was untenable for everyone, but especially for the vice and entertainment operators who were losing money every time they had to move. It wasn't long before they commenced returning to the old neighborhood and brought the new name with them, so that the downtown Tenderloin was now called the Uptown Tenderloin.

Reformers had long pressed the city fathers to clean up the city's vice districts. These were areas like the Barbary Coast; the brothels and gambling joints in the Chinatown alleys; and other vice districts like St. Mary's Place across from Old St. Mary's Church, and the Tenderloin. They now felt the sin-cleansing earthquake and fire had left San Francisco with a clean slate, an opportunity to start over, and they tried to get the city to rebuild these areas into respectable residential and business districts. But these plans were reckoned without consulting the property owners, many of whom had taken advantage of the nature of their tenants' activities in order to price rents at extortionate levels. When the denizens of the Uptown Tenderloin began returning to the old neighborhood, property owners jumped at the chance to resume business as usual, and a new hotel, entertainment, and vice district rose from the ashes of the old.

Anticipation of this outcome may have been one of the reasons why in 1907 the city included the neighborhood's first police station as well as a Hall of Justice with its jail and courts in its new, temporary City Hall right in the heart of the old Tenderloin on the site of the burned-out Tivoli Cafe on Eddy Street between Powell and Mason. The police court windows overlooked a cobblestone alley called Anna Lane and during the ensuing five years the judges complained bitterly about the racket made by wagons with iron-shod wheels rattling along the one-block thoroughfare.

Reconstruction in the Uptown Tenderloin was slow compared to other parts of what was called the burnt district. Most property owner's insurance plans covered the wood frame buildings that had been a ubiquitous feature of the Tenderloin before the fire, and they were insured for relatively small amounts. Then the city began instituting building codes requiring far more expensive fireproof construction. In addition to the difficulties this created for property owners to raise funds to rebuild, many owners decided to wait and see when the area would redevelop enough to attract new businesses, residents, and customers. Large sections of the old neighborhood, especially in its west half, remained partially or wholly undeveloped. When a decision was made in 1912 by San Francisco's politicians and businessmen to accelerate development by staging the Panama Pacific International Exposition in 1915, it set off a building boom in the east half of the Tenderloin, causing property owners to rebuild hotels and storefronts in time for the expected deluge of visitors.

Theaters were also rebuilt, although they moved north from between Eddy and O'Farrell streets to between Ellis and Geary. This led to some high-end hostelries that counted on the return of the theater trade when they rebuilt in the southeast corner of the Uptown Tenderloin to lower their aspirations and to start accommodating a more mid-priced clientele.

The new sensation of silent films became popular in San Francisco, as well as the rest of the country, and movie theaters were built primarily along Market Street as well as in outlying neighborhoods. This made the Uptown Tenderloin the center of the local film industry, mainly because most industry support services such as film makers, talent agents, film distributors, equipment retailers, repair shops, musicians, and actors and actresses were located in the neighborhood to be close to the Market Street theaters. Another less visible industry was the making of pornographic slides, photos, and films for exhibition and distribution at lodge "smokers" and other venues.

During this period, the city's political winds kept changing direction, first with a reform administration, then with a more relaxed administration, then with another reform administration and so on. One of the consequences was that the rules governing Uptown Tenderloin businesses went back and forth from law enforcement to lax enforcement. But the overall reformist trend, which had swept the rest of the United States, was much in evidence. Thus, there were numerous scandals and raisings and lowerings of the proverbial lid—until the onset of America's involvement in World War I.

In 1877, the completion of the Baldwin Hotel with its Academy of Music (on the right in photo), and the St. Ann's Building across Powell Street (on the left in photo), proclaimed the beginning of the transformation of the neighborhood from a residential neighborhood to a hotel, entertainment, and vice district. The intersection of Market, Powell, and Eddy streets, with these two structures, was seen as a gateway to Union Square and to Nob Hill where Leland Stanford built its first mansion the year before. At the time no one imagined it would become the entrance to a Tenderloin district. The photo was taken between 1879 and 1883. [*Private collector*]

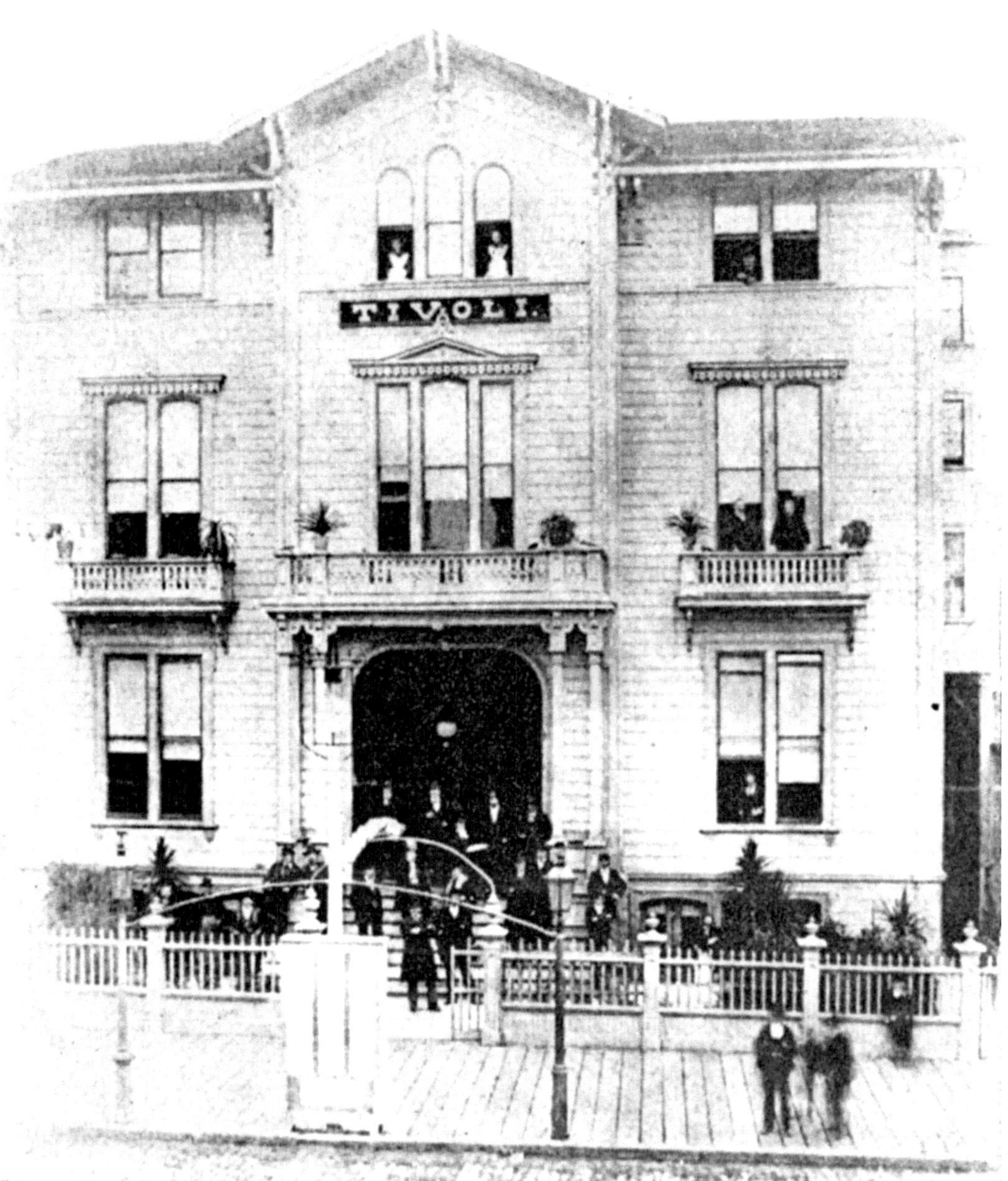

Joseph Kreling and his brothers moved their *Biergarten*, called the Tivoli Gardens, to gun-dealer Adolphus J. Plate's property, shown here on the north side of Eddy Street between Powell and Mason (now the Hilton Parc 55 Hotel) in 1879 after the building at the previous at Sutter and Stockton streets burned down. The new venue continued to show attractions like the Vienna Ladies Orchestra and the Spanish Students twenty-man mandolin and banjo orchestra, serving its standard fare of beer for the men and raspberry sodas for the ladies. [*Bancroft Library*]

Poor attendance decided the Kreling brothers to try light opera. They cobbled together the best players from several stranded troupes that had been presenting Gilbert and Sullivan's *HMS Pinafore*, still popular with American audiences, and remodeled the Tivoli into the neighborhood's second theater. *Pinafore* and other light operas enjoyed full houses there for years. In the 1880s the theater added an annual season of grand opera, which was also successful. After the opening of Baldwin's Academy of Music and the Tivoli Gardens, the old downtown theater districts were eclipsed by more theaters opening along O'Farrell, Geary, Powell, and Eddy streets. [*Pacific Coast Musical Review*]

Moses Gunst (far left) owned a retail tobacco business when he moved into The Arcade around 1880, a lodging house on Market Street next door to the Baldwin Hotel. He expanded his business into several Tenderloin and downtown branches, became a millionaire, and got himself appointed to the Police Commission, mostly to make sure businesses that attracted drinking and cigar smoking men such as saloons, cafes, concert halls, bookmakers, card clubs, and brothels wouldn't be bothered by reformers and politicians. [*Author's collection*]

The Wigwam Theater That Is to Be Removed to Make Room for the Spring Valley Building.

The lot that City College once stood on at the southeast corner of Stockton and Geary streets (now Neiman Marcus) was vacant for a decade until the San Francisco Republican Party built one of its wigwams—the nineteenth-century name for a temporary structure used for political rallies—on this site for the Cleveland-Blaine campaign in 1884. It had a tarred corrugated iron roof and was notorious for its poor ventilation in the summer and its cold temperatures in the winter. Over the next several years it alternated uses as a Republican rally hall and a theater variously named the Wigwam Garden and the Wigwam Garden Theatre but called the Wigwam Theater by the public and the media. [*San Francisco Call*]

Jimmy "Old Man" Hope was one the nineteenth century's most famous bank cracksmen. He learned his trade by working for a safe manufacturer, and no vault was safe in his presence. He was also an accomplished escape artist who had fled from every lockup he'd ever been placed in. But in 1881, while he was staying at a rooming house on Geary Street between Powell and Mason (now the former site of Lefty O'Doul's), he was caught drilling into the top of the vault of the Sather Bank. A clerk had complained about finding plaster dust from the ceiling on his desk every morning and suspicious bank officials called the police. Hope was convicted and sentenced to San Quentin, which turned out to be escape-proof for him. When he was released, he was met by New York detectives who took him back east to serve out the rest of his sentence from one of his previous prison breaks. [*Dark and Tangled Threads of Crime by William B. Secrest, courtesy of Linden Publishing, Inc.*]

The Beth Israel Synagogue was built in 1879 on the south side of Turk Street between Taylor and Jones (now Aunt Charlie's Lounge) after its congregation had been worshiping in various rental halls since 1861. Thirty years later the congregation sold the synagogue and the new owner remodeled it into The Temple; a concert hall and theater. But it wasn't a success and the building was auctioned off the following year. It became the headquarters and meeting hall of dozens of union locals and several Socialist political parties. For years many of San Francisco's strikes and other union activities were planned in this building, making the Tenderloin a center of union organizing in the city. [*The Morning Call/San Francisco Call*]

Michael H. De Young, owner of the *San Francisco Chronicle*, built the Alcazar Theatre on the north side of O'Farrell Street between Stockton and Powell (now Macy's). It opened on November 16, 1885 with a performance by American opera singer Emma Nevada. [*San Francisco History Center, San Francisco Public Library*]

Gustave Walter built the first Orpheum Theatre on O'Farrell Street between Stockton and Powell, directly across from M. H. De Young's Alcazar. It was a modest two-story building so lacking in distinction that the newspapers never published an image of it. Yet, it was large enough to seat 3,500 people. Walter, no businessman, partnered with Morris Meyerfeld after he nearly lost the theater. The association was so successful that they were able to expand into a chain of theaters and compete with other vaudeville circuits such as Keith-Albee. By the time Walter and Meyerfeld rebuilt their flagship San Francisco theater on a much grander scale in 1910, they had venues all over the west. Until recently, no image of the original theatre before the 1906 earthquake and fire was known to exist. [*Glenn Koch*]

Opposite above: The building housing the Alhambra Theater was built in 1890 on the northeast corner of Eddy and Jones streets (now Boeddeker Park) as another Republican wigwam to replace the one at Geary and Stockton in time to hold rallies for the California gubernatorial race. After hosting Republican political events for several years, it was leased by several unsuccessful theatrical producers from 1894 until it was remodeled into the Alhambra Theater by impresario Will Greenbaum four years later. Despite its out of the way location, it was successful until it was destroyed by the 1906 earthquake and fire. This photograph was taken around late spring or early summer of 1905. [*Glenn Koch Collection*]

Below: Harry Corbett, a brother of heavyweight champion Gentleman Jim Corbett and Major League Baseball star and sports writer Joe Corbett, opened a saloon and sports book in 1891 on the south side of Ellis Street between Stockton and Powell (see the sign on the three-story building on the left, now a parking lot). Corbett became a nationally known racing and boxing oddsmaker and referee. He had his own set of scales standing on an expensive Turkish carpet surrounded by a mahogany railing. When a boxer was invited to weigh in at Corbett's it was because there could be no question about the accuracy of the findings. At these times Ellis Street was made impassible by the throngs of sports trying to get a look at the fighter and waiting to hear the results so they could decide how to bet. [*Author's collection*]

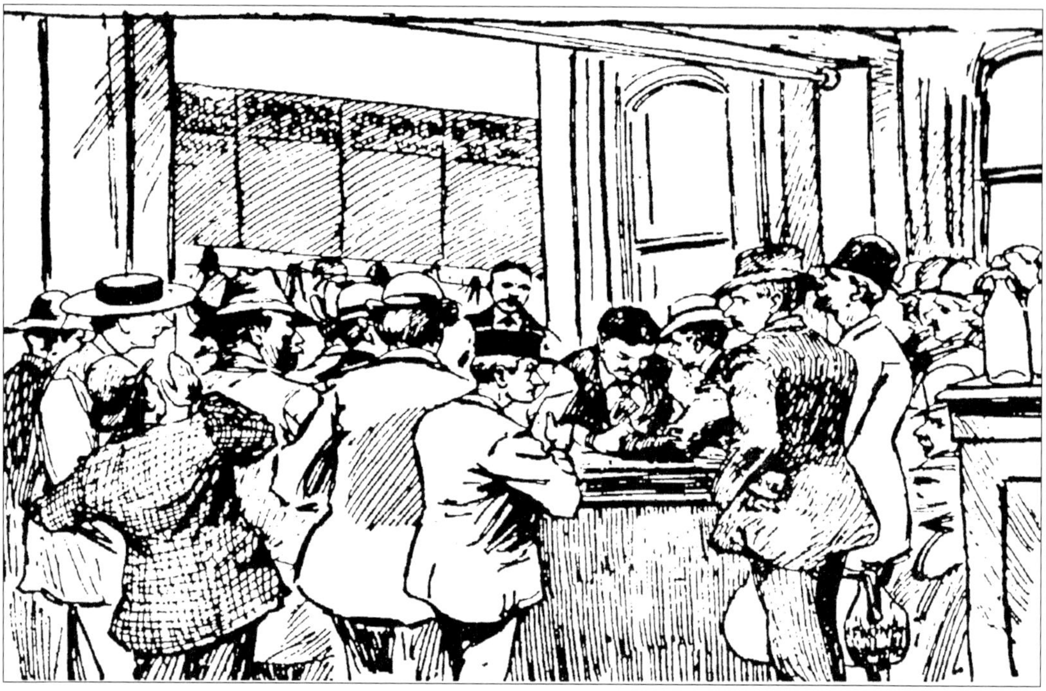

Ellis Street became a bookmaking district when other bookies moved there to take advantage of the business Corbett's was attracting. The venues were called poolrooms, and this drawing shows one of them. Corbett and other operators worked under the legal fiction that they were merely taking commissions from bets placed by the public, while passing the wagers on to trackside bookmakers. Of course, these off-track bookmakers never did any such thing and instead kept the bets. [*San Francisco Chronicle*]

A "LOOKOUT" FOR THE DOWN-TOWN POOLROOMS WATCHES THE RACES FROM AFAR.

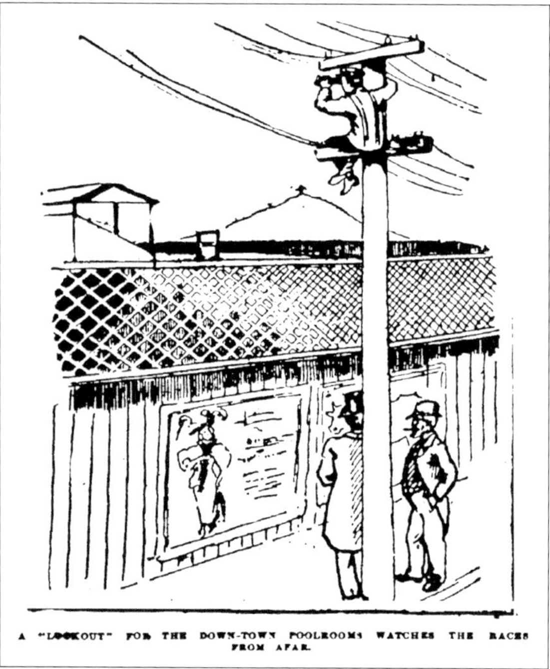

In those years the race tracks did what they could to undermine the downtown competition to their trackside books. This included denying access to information about race results, forcing the off-track bookmakers to resort to more or less devious intelligence gathering methods like the one in this newspaper illustration. The man with the binoculars would ride a bicycle to the nearest telegraph office to send in the results, or he would send a confederate. The race track detectives weren't above stealing the bicycles or arresting the observers. [*San Francisco Chronicle*]

THE WOMAN'S GAMBLING CLUB AT 11 ELLIS STREET.
[Sketched by a "Call" artist.]

But what really got the public stirred up was when several of the pool sellers decided there was an untapped market of female gamblers and opened at least six women-only books, causing the newspapers to deluge the public with stories asking if husbands knew how their wives were spending their days or how they were managing the household budget. [*San Francisco Chronicle, San Francisco Call*]

New York City Police Inspector Alexander "Clubber" Williams was the basis of an urban legend about how the Tenderloin got its name. New York newspapers claimed it was invented when Williams was assigned to command the precinct containing Manhattan's silk-stocking hotel, entertainment, and vice district, called Satan's Circus, with all the graft that came with it. When asked how he liked his new assignment, he was alleged to have answered, "I have had chuck for a long time, and now I'm going to eat tenderloin."[5] Newspapers across the continent began using the word to describe their vice districts, including San Francisco, where it stuck. [*Harper's New Monthly Magazine*]

Pete Dorcy was one of those saloon owners whose business depended largely on their reputations as local characters. In his case, it was about his luck in winning thousands of dollars on long-shot horse racing bets. The caption below the drawing referred to drinking establishments with side entrances for women (shown here), called "side-entrance saloons" at a time when only *demimondaines* would enter one of these places. [*San Francisco Call*]

Lord Sholto Douglas, the youngest son of the "pursuer of Oscar Wilde" (that is, the Ninth Marquess of Queensberry) and a brother of Lord Alfred Douglas who was pursued by Wilde, was traveling across America "to see the elephant." He found himself in Bakersfield, California in the spring of 1895 where he fell in love with a singer, one Loretta Mooney, at a theater performance. His marriage proposal was accepted, after which he was promptly jailed by his friends for three days on the assumption that he had lost his mind—but it was really to sober up and reconsider. He came to San Francisco and lodged at The Lexington on the north side of Eddy Street between Taylor and Jones (now the Hotel Windsor). Meanwhile, Miss Mooney also came to San Francisco to perform just a block away at the Auditorium Theater and visited Douglas at his hostelry. He waffled on the engagement, claiming it was lager rather than love that made him propose to her. Terrified the newspaper reports would cause his family to cut off his remittances, he telegraphed his relatives for more funds. In the meantime, he went to several races and occupied front row seats in several chorus shows. He then acknowledged the engagement, telegraphed his family again for funds and permission to marry the lady, while he also complained to reporters about all the media attention. When his pleas for resources and family blessings went unanswered, he married Mooney anyway in San Jose. [*San Francisco Chronicle*]

San Francisco before the fire had its share of noted professors of mixology like Jerry Thomas and Duncan Nichols. Among these first-rank stars was the relentlessly self-promoting William T. "Cocktail" Boothby, former Palace Hotel bartender and author of two mixology books. The image is an 1895 cut from *The Illustrated Directory* showing the Parker House saloon where Boothby presided, as he also did during Prohibition at the Olympic Club. [*California State Library*]

In the late nineteenth and early twentieth centuries, the Tenderloin and South of the Slot were where many of San Francisco's spiritualists, clairvoyants, psychic readers, astrologers, and similar practitioners lived and set up shop. One could turn onto Mason Street from Market in April 1906, just before the earthquake and fire, and see the palm of a hand painted on a second-story window (left side of the photo) with a drawing of a head on a sign nailed onto the frame, announcing the services of a palm-reader and phrenologist in his or her lodgings at The Metropole on the northwest corner of Mason and Turk streets (current site of the Hotel Metropolis and farmerbrown). [*Bancroft Library*]

The building on the near right on the southeast corner of O'Farrell and Powell streets (now the Elevated Shops building) was where well-known Tenderloin madam Tessie Wall opened her first parlor house in 1897, just up the block from the Orpheum Theatre and across the street from Fischer's Theatre and the Alcazar. By 1900, Mrs. Wall moved across the street to the southwest corner, where she either set up her operation or took one over from "Mrs. Magdalena Morton." She stayed at this location until the 1906 earthquake and fire. The photograph was taken in 1905. [*Western Neighborhoods Project/Private collector*]

Isaac W. Bain was a confidence man who specialized in marriage bureau fraud. In 1897 he was located at 110 Ellis Street between Powell and Mason (now the Hotel Fusion). He placed advertisements in newspapers across the country saying, "a pretty 20-year-old heiress is in trouble: a large sum is offered to any respectable man that will marry her,"[6] and inviting men to contact his Pacific Information and Introduction Bureau. The post office inspectors and the police got wind of him, and this, combined with newspaper exposures, forced him to close up shop. He resurfaced six months later with a female accomplice who lived in a lodging house at 415 Jones Street between O'Farrell and Geary (now the Aldrich Hotel). He used her to entice a Pennsylvania man to come to San Francisco with $2,000 on the promise of marriage. [*San Francisco Call*]

The Admission Day Monument was sculpted by Douglas Tilden and originally installed by the city in 1897 at the intersection of Market, Mason, and Turk streets to commemorate the date of California's statehood. For fifty years it was the Tenderloin's only statue. In 1948 it had become an obstruction to plans for changing the neighborhood's traffic pattern from two-way to one-way thoroughfares and was moved to Golden Gate Park. It is now at the intersection of Market, Montgomery, and Post streets. The photograph is dated 1912. That's the Ambassador Hotel being constructed at the left on the southwest corner of Mason and Eddy streets. [*Western Neighborhoods Project/Private collector*]

The Tragedy on the Threshold of the Empire Theater.

Above left: Dolly Ogden was a Tenderloin parlor house madam. She distributed tokens as a marketing tool to likely referral sources such as hack drivers, bartenders, bell hops, headwaiters, barbers, shoeshine stand operators, newsstand operators, or anyone else a gentleman was likely to ask for information about where to have a good time. The gentleman would be brought to the parlor house by the referent. If he bought champagne, which was the usual custom, the next day the referral source would receive a red envelope with a ten percent kickback. [*Jerry F. Schimmel/Therese Van Wiele*]

Above right: The front of the token advertised Ogden's house at 326 Mason Street between O'Farrell and Geary (now a liquor store and a Lori's Diner). The motto on the back of the coin translates to "all the same" or "always the same." [*Jerry F. Schimmel/Therese Van Wiele*]

Opposite page: In the 1890s, the Tenderloin started to get a little rough. For example, in 1898 former Visalia bartender Charles E. Weathers shot and killed Nathan Phillips—an innocent bystander walking out of the basement entrance to a concert saloon called the Empire Theater on Ellis Street between Stockton and Powell (now the Converse store)—when Weathers was trying to shoot the theater's cashier and several other employees, thinking he was at the Thalia Theater at Turk and Market streets. He was thrown out of the Thalia several hours earlier during a drinking spree, and then went to his room at the Royal Eagle at Powell and Ellis streets (now the Hotel Union Square) to get his pistol. He said the Thalia Theater had stolen twenty-dollars from him. He was carrying a letter from his brother in Visalia—where Weathers had shot a man two years before—imploring him to put away his pistol. [*San Francisco Chronicle*]

Alfred Techau heavily remodeled the old United Presbyterian Church on Henry Gerke's former lot on the west side of Mason Street between Eddy and Ellis (now a Glide Church family housing project) and opened his first Techau Tavern in 1899. Techau thought he could make money in the Tenderloin by offering a German version of a San Francisco-style French restaurant. In other words, a legitimate eatery with private dining and hotel rooms upstairs, and not too many questions if a gentleman and his lady looked respectable enough. [*San Francisco History Center/San Francisco Public Library*]

The Eureka Benevolent Society was a charitable organization formed in the 1850s to help needy German Jews in Gold Rush San Francisco. Over the years the society leased different offices around the city, several of them in the Tenderloin. In 1900, the society built its own offices (shown here) on O'Farrell Street between Taylor and Jones. After the 1906 earthquake and fire, the Society built this larger structure on the same lot around 1909 (now a fortune teller). The organization moved to the Western Addition in 1932 and is now the Jewish Family and Children's Service Agency. [*Author's collection*]

In 1902, the Police Commission ordered the transfer of several officers from the Tenderloin as part of a corruption probe which was reported in the newspapers. During that period the Chief of Police heard about a prostitute named Lulu Wilson complaining that Officer Alexander was extorting $2.50 a week from her in protection payments and also made her move to another lodging house, The Queen on Mason Street between Market and Eddy (now the Mikkeller Bar). The Chief arranged for the prostitute to make the next payment while he observed the transaction from a nearby restaurant window. He then confronted the officer and found him in possession of the marked coins used for the payoff. The officer was dismissed from the force. [*San Francisco Call*]

SPIDER KELLY PROMOTES JOY

Second Ball Calls Out Big Crowd of Members of His Social Set.

James Patrick "Spider Kelly" Curtin was a lightweight pugilist who earned seven wins, eight losses, and one tie between 1893 and 1901. He left the ring to open a saloon in 1902 or 1903, at first as a junior partner in a storefront under The Queen which was his lodging house on the east side of Mason Street between Market and Eddy (now the Bar Mikkeller). The following year he moved around the corner to Eddy Street between Market and Mason (now the Little Delhi restaurant) as the senior partner in his eponymously named saloon, where he reigned until the 1906 earthquake and fire. Kelly was a dis, dem, and dose guy who wore shoits instead of shirts. Say, for instance, some character was arrested for bouncing a check or getting into a fracas in his saloon. The next day Kelly would refuse to press charges at the police court, doubtless having already adjusted the matter privately. During his years on Eddy Street he presided over an annual social affair for the "Members of his Social Set." The newspaper article about his 1904 event characterized the balls as serving a similar function to Chuck Conner's "rackets" in New York's Bowery—the latter luminary having sent a congratulatory telegram to Kelly, although Kelly claimed Connors' functions were too rough compared to his. [*San Francisco Chronicle*]

This Unconvicted Felon Struggling to Escape From the Quagmire of His Own Crimes.

By the time Christopher A. Buckley moved in 1901 or 1902 from Pacific Heights to the old Mackay mansion on O'Farrell Street between Larkin and Polk (now the Great American Music Hall), he had been driven out of politics for close to a decade and divided his time between his Tenderloin mansion and his estate in the Livermore Valley. This was his reward for being the San Francisco Democratic Party boss in the 1880s and early 1890s. He achieved this level of political influence by opening a saloon and cultivating friendships and influence through the customers he met there. Never running for political office himself, he supervised the Democratic Party from the back room of his Alhambra saloon on lower Bush Street in the classic style of nineteenth and early twentieth century political bosses. He reorganized the fractured Democratic Party so skillfully that it won several elections. He was called the Blind Boss after he lost his eyesight in the 1870s and became adept at remembering people by their handshakes, memorizing deals, recalling legislation, and keeping track of political favors and patronage, through which he became rich. [*Author's collection/San Francisco Examiner*]

By the time this photograph was taken of the southwest corner of Geary and Stockton streets in Union Square in 1905, many of its residential homes were replaced by businesses and the only residential structures left were rooming houses, hotels, and offices. [*San Francisco History Center/ San Francisco Public Library*]

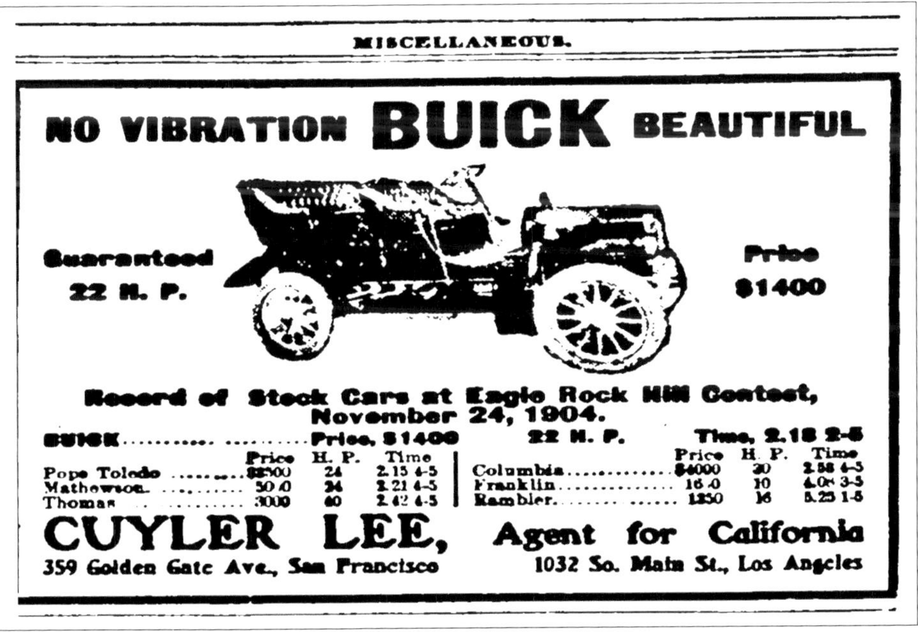

In 1905, there were only a few automobile dealers in San Francisco. This was before Henry Ford brought mass production to the industry; automobiles were still a relatively expensive toy primarily for wealthy enthusiasts. These dealers located in the southwest corner of the Tenderloin along the section of Golden Gate Avenue that later became Auto Row. [*San Francisco Chronicle*]

The Colonial Theatre was built on the north side of McAllister Street between Jones and Leavenworth (now the Dorothy Day Community senior housing project) and was the first permanent performance venue to open after the earthquake and fire, mostly because it was nearly finished when the 1906 conflagration gutted the interior but left the shell intact. It opened on October 6, with Frank Bacon starring in Henry A. Du Souchet's *The Man from Mexico*. [*San Francisco History Center/San Francisco Public Library*]

Opposite above: The Belvedere (in the intact five-story building with the arches on the windows of the second and fourth floors) was a basement cafe in a building constructed by a consortium of Tenderloin cafe owners and boxing and horse racing promoters such as Eddie Graney and James Coffroth. It prided itself on providing an escort to the Hammam Baths around the corner on Grant Avenue for any man too inebriated to navigate his way home. The photograph was taken on the day of the earthquake, April 18, 1906. [*Bancroft Library*]

Opposite below: Market and Eddy streets after the 1906 earthquake and fire. The corner entrance with the stairs and the word "TELEPHONE" on one of the supports is part of what little remained of the St. Ann's Building (now the Forever 21 store and the Lofts at One Powell). [*San Francisco Chronicle*]

A number of temporary structures were built in the "burnt district" after the 1906 earthquake and fire, including in the Tenderloin. One of them was the saloon and cigar shop of San Francisco historian Emiliano Echeverria's grandfather, Christian Karsten, at 701 O'Farrell Street on the southwest corner of Hyde (now the Hyde & O'Farrell Market), which he opened sometime between May and September of 1906. (Karsten is behind the counter on the left.) After operating a grocery store before the catastrophe, he decided there was money to be made selling beer and stogies to the hordes of men working in the Tenderloin during the rebuilding. [*Emiliano Echeverria*]

Opposite above: A photograph of Mayor Eugene Schmitz (fifth person from the right) and the new 1906 Board of Supervisors. During the election, political boss Abe Ruef's Union Labor Party managed to re-elect Schmitz, and unexpectedly swept the Board of Supervisors seats. The newly elected supervisors were political neophytes who thought of their election in opportunistic terms and were so greedy for graft that Ruef warned Schmitz "they would eat the paint off a house,"[7] giving them their moniker, the Paint Eaters. They were amateurs, and their efforts to solicit bribes were so blatant that Ruef was forced to take charge of the boodling to prevent exposure. [*Bancroft Library*]

Right: This photograph shows Abe Ruef and one of his lawyers during the post-earthquake and fire graft prosecutions. The start of their downfall was when Ruef extorted payments from the owners of French restaurants, many of which were in the Tenderloin, in exchange for renewing their liquor permits. One of the restaurants happened to be the favorite dining spot of muckraking *San Francisco Call* editor Fremont Older, and the owner complained to him about the extortion scheme. This launched the *Call*'s investigation and led to the prosecution of Ruef, Schmitz, and the Paint Eaters. [*Bancroft Library*]

Relative to the rest of San Francisco, the area from the Uptown Tenderloin to Nob Hill was slow to rebuild after the 1906 earthquake and fire. But the February 3, 1907 *San Francisco Chronicle* reported the completion of the Hotel Hamlin on the south side of Eddy Street between Jones and Leavenworth, and said it was the first permanent downtown hotel to be built after the fire. Other hotels, such as the Landa (shown next door on the corner) and the Hotel Allen (shown on the far corner), were completed later that year, while the Cadillac Hotel (not shown, but directly across Eddy Street from the Hamlin) was completed in March or April of 1908. [*California State Library*]

William "Doc" Leahy, manager of the destroyed Tivoli Opera and a member of the Police Commission, offered to lease to the city the building he was constructing on the site of the original Tivoli Opera on the north side of Eddy Street between Powell and Mason (now the Hilton Parc 55 Hotel) for use as a temporary city hall. This is how the city came to administer and govern San Francisco from the Uptown Tenderloin District from early 1907 through early 1912, when the new Hall of Justice was completed on Kearny Street and the city offices moved there. (The building is the nearest two-story structure.) [*OpenSFHistory/Private collector*]

The Cadillac Hotel on the northeast corner of Eddy and Leavenworth streets was completed in March or April of 1908 for Andrew Louderback, who owned and lived on the property from at least as far back as 1858 up until the 1906 earthquake and fire. It was one of many new hotels near Market Street that had to adjust their expectations downward to a more mid-priced clientele when most of the theaters rebuilt farther north on O'Farrell and Geary streets. [*San Francisco History Center/San Francisco Public Library*]

Many post-earthquake and fire Uptown Tenderloin lodging houses were built to be only two or three-stories high on narrow lots, replacing single-family or double-fronted wood frame structures which were insured for relatively small amounts based on their modest value. After the disaster, the city began enforcing stricter building codes requiring fire-proof construction, which required more expensive construction materials like brick, reinforced concrete, and steel. Because the insurance settlements for the original buildings typically covered only a fraction of the cost of new construction, property owners had to borrow money to rebuild. As was often or usually the case, their only collateral was the lot itself and so the size of a loan was generally limited to the value of the lot, which in turn restricted the size of the buildings. However, it turned out that these small building sizes were ideal for brothels, and this is what they were often used for. This one on Turk Street between Taylor and Jones (now the Boston Hotel and the City Impact Rescue Mission) was built by architect Charles M. Rousseau in 1908 as The Wilson lodging house. In the days of the Uptown Tenderloin, the storefront was used as a bookie joint and the lodging house above it was operated as a brothel by Mary (or Marie) Raymond, typical for buildings of this type. The photograph is dated 1914. [*Glenn Koch Collection*]

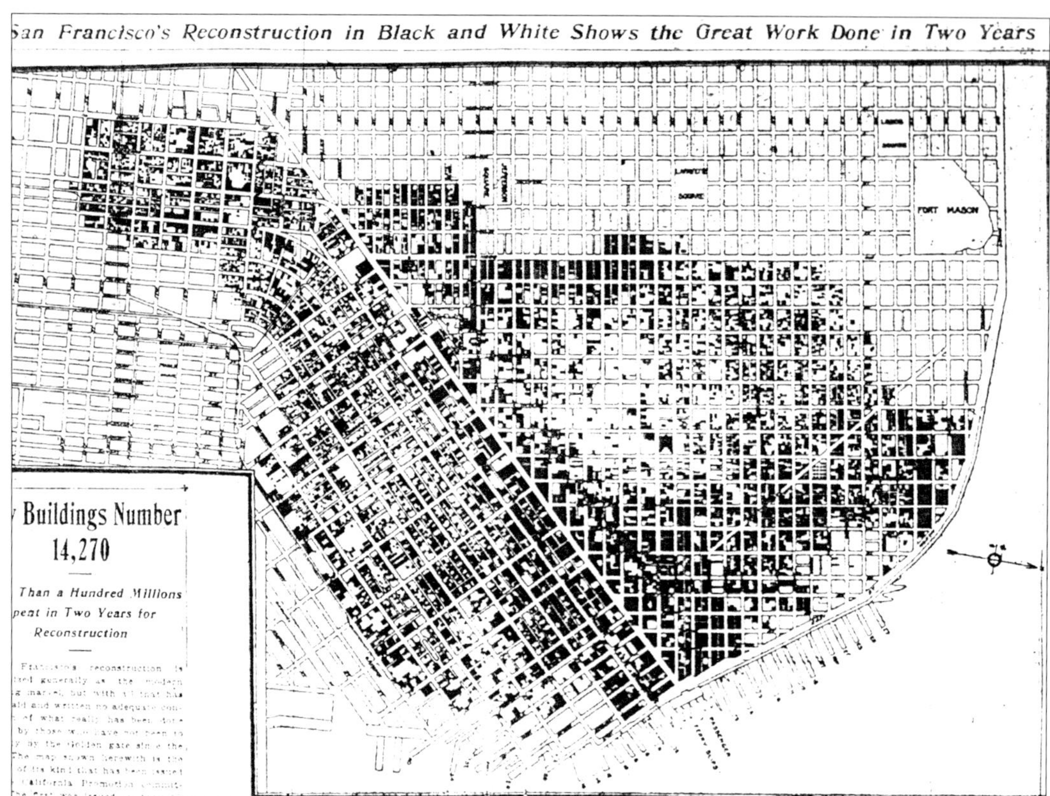

By April 1908, San Francisco's recovery from the earthquake and fire was well on its way. But in Nob Hill and the Uptown Tenderloin, redevelopment was still spotty and the area between the two was almost a desert. [*San Francisco Call*]

In his time, which was throughout the 1890s up to World War I, Jerome Bassity (upper left in the photograph) was one of the vice operators most responsible for the corruption that pervaded the Tenderloin. He owned the Coronado saloon on the southwest corner of Mason and Ellis streets (now The Old Siam Thai restaurant) from the 1890s, while his brother Neil dealt drugs from the saloon safe. He owned or had controlling interests in several brothels in the Uptown Tenderloin and in Chinatown after the fire. He was a partner in a Sacramento enterprise that broke in new prostitutes by having a doctor sever their Fallopian tubes so there wouldn't be any down time from pregnancies, while also using their subsequent pain to addict the women to drugs they had to buy from the house. He owned the Haymarket Music Hall, a dive in the basement of the building that housed his saloon where he employed "pretty waiter girls." It was so depraved that most prostitutes refused to work there. He got away with all this by getting out the vote in the Tenderloin and donating to political campaigns. This resulted in his operations rarely ever being closed down, even when the lid was down. [*San Francisco Call*]

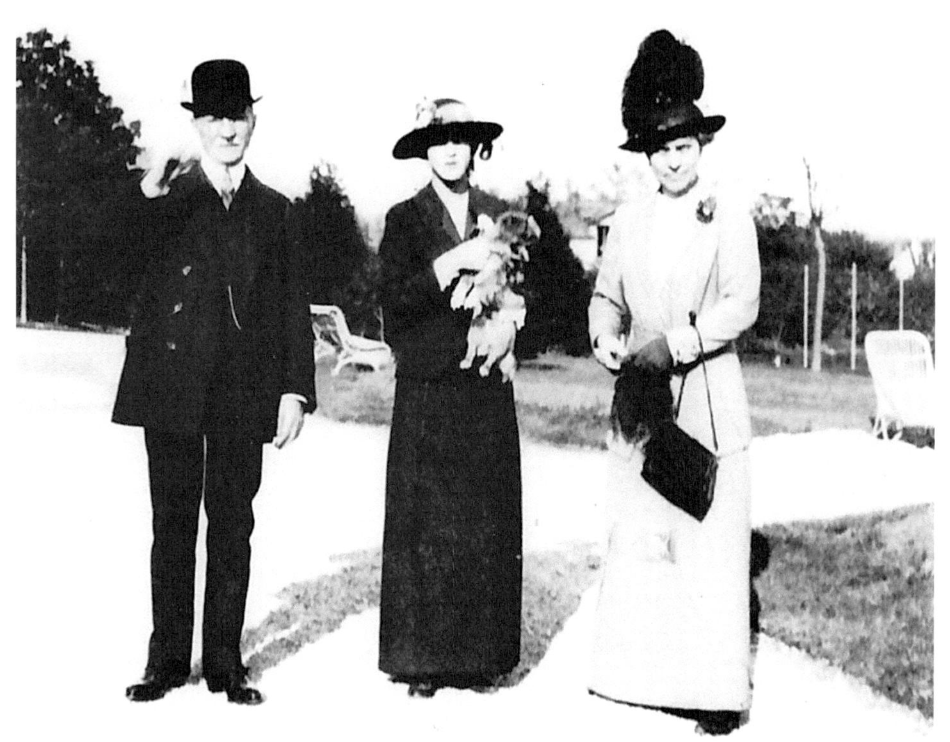

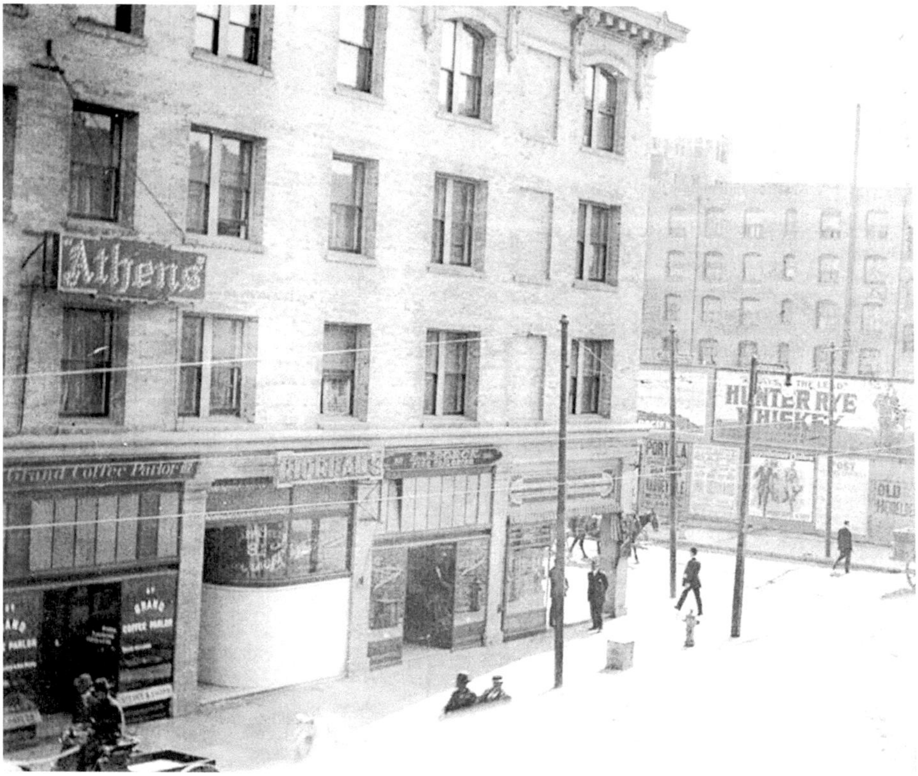
Athens
Grand Coffee Parlor
GRAND COFFEE PARLOR
HUNTER RYE
OLD

Sandy McNaughton was a well-known Uptown Tenderloin sport who loved horse racing and boxing. He opened a branch of his Breakers Cafe in the basement of the Hotel Athens as soon as it was built. But he closed it down within months when the Police Commission threatened to revoke his liquor license if he didn't stop the music and dancing that were featured there, which at that time were illegal in saloons outside the boundaries of the Barbary Coast. [*Glenn Koch Collection*]

Opposite above: Alex W. Wilson was a Swedish immigrant who bought several Tenderloin properties in the prosperous southeast corner of the neighborhood in the 1890s and made a small fortune leasing buildings for cafes and lodging houses. Shown in the photograph are Wilson, his wife Rose, and their daughter Berenice. [*Jacob Schurman*]

Opposite below: After the 1906 earthquake and fire, Wilson rebuilt his properties. These included the Hotel Athens on the southwest corner of Mason and Eddy streets (later the Hotel Bristol), shown here after its completion in 1909. After his death, his wife Rose ran the family business, which the family kept for several generations until the 1960s and 1970s when declining rents and property values caused them to sell out. [*Bancroft Library*]

The next basement tenant of the Athens Hotel was John Crowley, who opened the Black Cat restaurant there in late 1911, shown here in this whimsical postcard. It stayed open until early 1921 when it was one of the cafes shut down by the Police Commission for allowing dancing without a permit. The owner opened another cafe in the same location called Old Madrid, but the Commission also shut that one down for the same reason. [*Glenn Koch Collection*]

Opposite page: In 1909, Uptown Tenderloin madams Tessie Wall and Pearl Morton opened parlor houses next door to each other at 337 and 339 O'Farrell Street between Mason and Taylor (now the Hilton Hotel). Miss Morton's five-story building is shown, with just a corner of Mrs. Wall's peeking out from under the photograph of an unrelated structure. These were especially discrete locations for parlor houses because they both had rear entrances from a small alley called Dikeman Place running west from Mason Street. [*San Francisco Examiner*]

TARAVELLIER BUILDING

Frank Daroux was an Uptown Tenderloin gambling czar who was one of the people in charge of collecting tribute from neighborhood vice operations for the Republican Party. Tessie Wall met him at a dinner where he was said to have been amazed at her ability to drink bottle after bottle of champagne without once leaving the table. Being a gambler, he knew there was a trick—one of a brothel madam's jobs was to get customers to order as much expensive champagne as possible—but what impressed him was that it was so smoothly done that he couldn't figure it out. They became a couple, but because of his political ambitions he wouldn't marry her unless it was in secret. And he wanted her to give up the brothel business and move to a home he was going to build in San Mateo. Tessie famously said, "San Mateo! Why I'd sooner be under one electric light on Powell Street than to own all of San Mateo!"[8] Their relationship went back and forth for years until Daroux finally separated from her. She would wait for him to appear on the street and try to talk him into a reconciliation. One day, as they were turning from Ellis Street onto Anna Lane, Daroux said something particularly wounding to Wall and she pulled out her derringer pistol and shot him. When asked why she did this, she replied, "I shot him 'cause I love him, Goddamn him."[9] Daroux survived the shooting but moved to New York. Wall was acquitted of the shooting and retired to the Mission District. [*San Francisco Call*]

The Adams Cosmopolitan School was rebuilt after the 1906 earthquake and fire on its old site on Eddy between Polk Street and Van Ness Avenue (now the City College of San Francisco Civic Center Campus), first as a temporary wood frame structure in 1907, and then a permanent building in 1910 (shown here). Enrollment was so high that an annex was built on Ellis Street behind the school. It was the only Tenderloin school to be rebuilt. [*San Francisco Public Library/San Francisco History Center*]

Until 1916, according to *The Wasp*, Coffee Dan's, located in the basement of the building on the northeast corner of O'Farrell and Powell streets, was just another ham 'n' egger, a basement restaurant for the local workers, until "Some ingenious and popular belle suggested a visit to the place, by way of deviltry ... That night the quietude of Coffee Dan's habitat was assailed by a limousine ... A night or so later, another courageous group, satiated with the humdrum of dancing found its way down the narrow stairs ere parting for the night." Within a week there wasn't even standing room–Coffee Dan's had been discovered. It "became the rendezvous of San Francisco's elite! All the fair and fashionable were there, for an hour or so after the theaters were out ... and the reputation of Dan, *Coffee* Dan, took wings on the wave of a brand-new fad!"[10] It is now a Skechers store. [*Glenn Koch Collection*]

John Davis, the son of the founder, seems to have run with Coffee Dan's, expanding it into a night club with entertainment, and in no time at all it was being featured in plays, movies, and books. During Prohibition it was one of San Francisco's best-known speakeasies. This 1925 photograph shows the Tenderloin when Coffee Dan's was still hot. Starting in 1910, the building also housed the Kingston Club card room on the second floor. Gambling greats like Joe "Silver Fox" Bernstein and Eddie Sahati played high stakes poker there, sometimes for pots as high as $35,000. [*Western Neighborhood Project/ Emiliano Echeverria/Randolph Brandt Collection*]

The first Columbia Theatre opened in 1895 on Powell Street between Eddy and Ellis (now the Axiom Hotel). Like other theaters in the old Tenderloin, it moved north after the earthquake and fire, in this case to Geary Street between Mason and Taylor (current site of the American Conservatory Theater's Geary Theater). It first opened with George Ade's *Father and the Boys* in January 1910. [*San Francisco History Center/San Francisco Public Library*]

Dave Becker, the cafe owner, who was killed yesterday morning in an automobile accident on the Great Highway, and two young women who were among the passengers in the machine at the time of the disaster, receiving a number of injuries.

According to Jack Tillmany in *Theatres of San Francisco*, the second Alcazar Theatre was designed by architects Cunningham and Politeo and was built on O'Farrell Street between Powell and Mason (now the O'Farrell Street side of the Handlery Union Square Hotel), a block west of the original theater. It opened to a sold-out house on December 23, 1911 with Patterson and Ford's *The Fourth Estate*. It was operated by several different theatrical impresarios over the years. [*San Francisco History Center/San Francisco Public Library*]

Opposite page: Dave Becker operated a saloon on the northwest corner of Mason and Turk streets (now the Hotel Metropole and the farmerbrown restaurant) before the earthquake and fire. After the disaster, he relocated to the Uptown Tenderloin in the Western Addition but returned downtown in 1910 to a new cafe at 166 Eddy Street between Mason and Taylor in a storefront in the Hotel Kern (now the William Penn Hotel and the Exit Theater). Becker was killed in 1911 in an automobile accident while driving late at night along the Great Highway with another friend and two Uptown Tenderloin women. [*San Francisco Chronicle*]

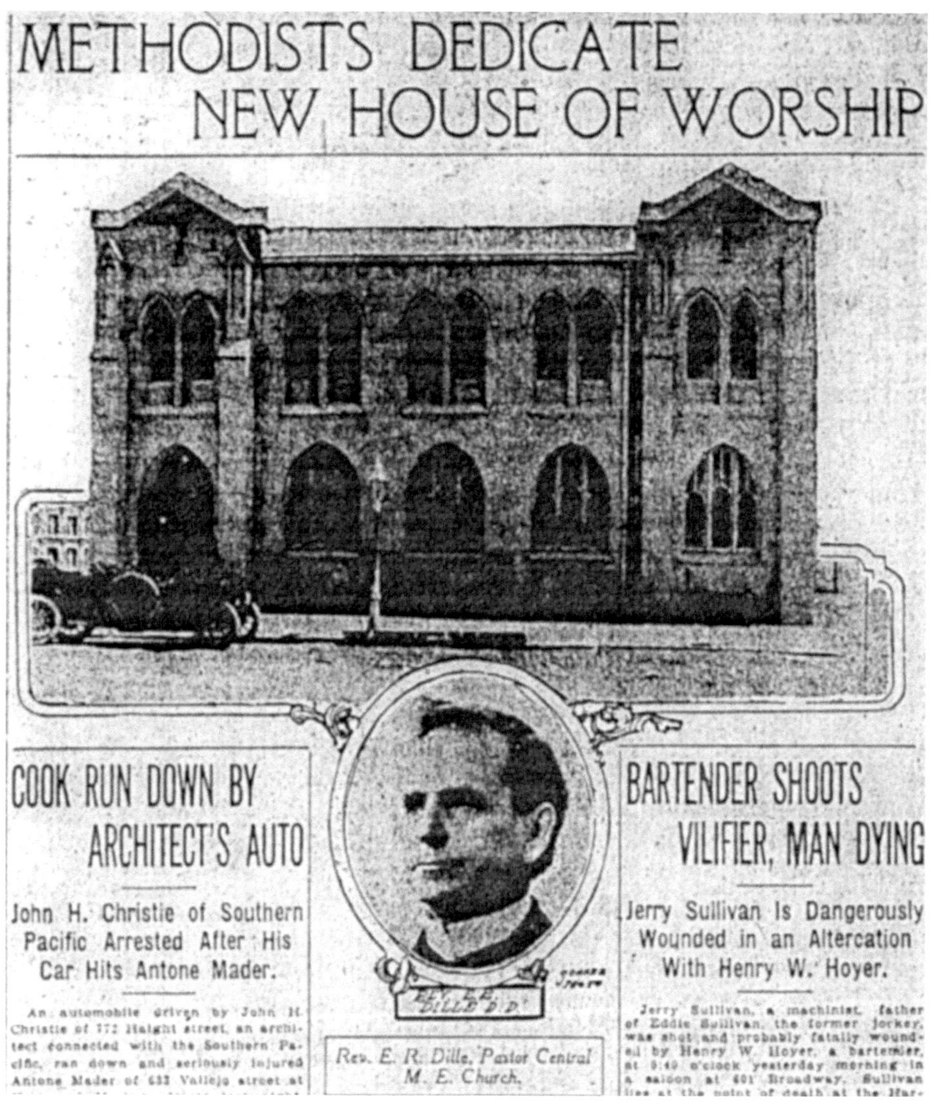

Rev. E. R. Dille, Pastor Central M. E. Church.

In 1911 the Central Methodist Episcopal Church rebuilt its house of worship, moving its location from Mission Street between Sixth and Seventh to the southwest corner of O'Farrell and Leavenworth streets (now the Farrellworth Apartments). In 1916 the church acquired a new pastor named Rev. Paul Smith. Unusually tall and a gifted speaker, he was outraged when one day a young male parishioner complained of being solicited by a prostitute on the street right in front of the church. Smith launched an anti-vice crusade that coincided with a reform campaign by a number of women's organizations, a concerted push by Union Square businesses and Tenderloin property owners to eliminate vice in order to expand the shopping district there, and the presence of a mayoral administration that got itself elected partly on promises to be responsive to the long-neglected needs of the neighborhoods of San Francisco. Sunny Jim Rolph preferred to live and let live when it came to vice, but when the people who voted for him agitated for a cleanup, he jumped in with both feet. [*San Francisco Chronicle*]

Rev. Smith was an effective politician, organizing the many reform groups under an umbrella organization led by himself, and exerting steady pressure on the Rolph administration that resulted in constant raids and arrests in the Uptown Tenderloin. There were three main outcomes. First, the California Supreme Court ruled in January 1917 that the Red Light Abatement Act, which had been passed and then challenged in court three years before, was constitutional, allowing Mayor Rolph to announce a full scale investigation leading to the closing down of all the San Francisco brothels. Second, Uptown Tenderloin parlor house madam Reggie Gamble showed up at Rev. Smith's church just days later with 300 prostitutes. She told him that if he was going to deprive them of their livelihoods, then he had to help them get decent paying jobs, which were difficult for women to find in those days. He responded with platitudes, and Gamble led the ladies out of the church, saying, "There's nothing for us here." (Read on for the third outcome.) [*San Francisco Bulletin*]

Thousands Pack Dreamland to Aid in War on Vice
Mass Meeting Demands Citizens' Committee

Minister Unable to Answer Woman's World-Old Question

Above: Antonio Blanco, who owned the Poodle Dog on the northeast corner of Mason and Eddy streets (now the Hilton Parc 55 Hotel) before the earthquake and fire, built a new restaurant in 1907 on the site of the old Mackay-O'Connor-Buckley mansion on O'Farrell Street between Larkin and Polk (now the Great American Music Hall), and apparently also leased the hotel next to it, calling the operation Blanco's Hotel & Restaurant. [*Glenn Koch Collection*]

Opposite above: The third consequence happened that same evening, when 7,000 people assembled at the Dreamland Rink in the Western Addition to listen to Rev. Smith's call for action to shut down vice in San Francisco. This degree of political pressure, coming directly from the people who put him in office, made Mayor Rolph order his Police Commission president, Theodore Roche, to close the lid on vice throughout the city. [*San Francisco Chronicle*]

Opposite below: The first St. Francis Theatre was completed around 1916 on the south side of Geary Street between Powell and Mason, one of many built during the early years of the silent movie craze. *Ashes of Embers* was produced in 1916 by the Famous Players Film Company, directed by Joseph Kaufman and Edward Jose, and is now lost. Pauline Frederick played twin sisters, one good and one bad. This site was later a Compton's Cafeteria branch and then the second site of Lefty O'Doul's hofbrau until it moved to Fisherman's Wharf in 2018. [*California State Library*]

Above: Blanco also reopened the Poodle Dog in 1910 on the north side of Mason Street between Eddy and Ellis where the first Techau Tavern had been located before the fire (now a Glide Church family housing project). Both enterprises did well until 1918, when the Poodle Dog was raided and Blanco was prosecuted for operating a house of ill fame. The charge was a libel: the French restaurants never ran brothels or provided women. They merely provided a location for assignations. However, the charge was dismissed only on his promise to retire from the hotel and restaurant business. [*San Francisco City Directory*]

Opposite above: Alfred Techau rebuilt his Techau Tavern on the prized northwest corner of Powell and Eddy streets in 1909 (now the Forever 21 store and the Lofts at One Powell). He kept it going until 1918 when the lot was sold out from under him to the Bank of Italy, which built its new headquarters there. [*Private collector*]

Opposite below: The German House, or *Das Deutsches Haus* as it was called by San Francisco's German-Americans, was built in 1912 by a consortium of forty-three German fraternal societies on the northwest corner of Polk and Turk streets (now an Academy of Art building), to fill the need of these organizations for a hall to conduct meetings, drill practices, celebrations, etc. It was designed by architect Frederich Meyer in the German Renaissance style based on Heidelberg Castle and on the Pellerhaus in Nurenberg. It was renamed California Hall around the time of World War I when it was used as an embarkation point for American troops. [*Author's collection*]

EUROPEAN
TECHAU TAVERN
FURNITURE MFRS. SAMPLE HOUSE
OLLEGE
TECHAU TAVERN

THE ACADEMY GRILL

The Knights of Columbus Hall was designed by architect Smith O'Brien and completed in 1912 on the south side of Golden Gate Avenue between Jones and Leavenworth. The International Longshoreman's and Warehouseman's Union occupied the building between 1948 and 1973. According to literary historian Don Herron, this was where Eric Hoffer got job assignments while he was writing *The True Believer* and also where Allen Ginsberg gave a reading of *Kaddish*. [*San Francisco History Center/San Francisco Public Library*]

The Larkin Theatre was built by architect William Knowles in 1916. It had a Wurlitzer organ and it showed a new silent feature every night, like Theda Bara vamping it up in "Sin," during its first month of business. The store next door sold Belgian candy, ice cream, and soft drinks and was a part of the theater for many years. [*Western Neighborhoods Project/Private collector*]

ENDNOTES

1. "Williams, 'Ex-Czar' of Tenderloin, Dies," *New York Times* (March 26, 1917)

2. "At Republican Headquarters," *The Evening World* (November 8, 1877), 1.

3. "A Curious Tenement," *San Francisco Chronicle* (November 26, 1888), 6. Reprint of "Capt. Reilly's Off Hours," *The Sun* (April 29, 1888), 3.

4. "Historic trail raised the bar for tipplers in S.F.," *San Francisco Chronicle* (December 14, 2013) C1.

5. "Williams, 'Ex-Czar' of Tenderloin, Dies," *New York Times* (March 26, 1917)

6. "They All Wanted the Indian Girl," *San Francisco Call* (October 4, 1897), 1.

7. Bean, Walton, *Boss Ruef's San Francisco* (Berkeley, University of California Press, 1972), 215.

8. Gentry, Curt, *The Madams of San Francisco* (Garden City, N. Y., Doubleday, 1964), 223.

9. *Ibid*, 210.

10. *The Wasp* (May 20, 1916), 11.

THREE

World War I, Prohibition, and The Great Depression

Up until the last two years of World War I, the Tenderloin and other San Francisco vice and entertainment districts, such as the Barbary Coast and Chinatown, were able to keep operating, albeit while fighting the waves of reform that had been sweeping San Francisco and the rest of the country since the nineteenth century. But in 1917, the United States' decision to mount an American Expeditionary Force and send it to Europe to fight in the war ran into a major hurdle: it was found that one out of every four servicemen were unfit for service because of alcoholism, drug addiction, or venereal disease. This was dealt with in the characteristically summary fashion of military emergencies: a series of decrees closed every brothel, saloon, and gambling joint located within five miles of any military base in the United States. In San Francisco, this encompassed over seventy percent of the city and included every vice district.

Until this time, appeals of the California Red Light Abatement Act (passed by the state legislature in 1913) meant the Act remained unenforced. But a California Supreme Court ruling exhausted those appeals and unleashed a wave of demands for vice suppression that sent politicians scrambling to enforce the Act as they ran for political cover, while a Federal war tax on alcoholic beverages was so high that restaurants and saloons stopped serving alcohol and stores stopped selling it. This created a *de facto* Prohibition for two years before the Eighteenth Amendment was ratified. The overall effect of these measures was to drive underground the vice operations that survived. San Francisco, like other large U.S. coastal cities in World War I, was swarming with servicemen, many of whom wanted a drink, a game of chance, and a woman. But with brothels no longer running openly—saloons, brothels, and gambling joints were no longer allowed to serve members of the military and were constantly raided besides—and the price of drinks becoming astronomical, it was more than just difficult for a serviceman to have a good time.

Prostitutes, instead of operating discreetly in brothels or on the streets, worked covertly out of hotels and apartments. Moreover, organizations like the YMCA were opening branches in places like the Uptown Tenderloin to offer sober recreational choices. The heat was on, and it stayed on throughout the war. But the reform movements lost much of their impetus over time and vice slowly returned to what was again being called just the Tenderloin in the first months after Armistice Day, though more surreptitiously than before America's entry into the war. Stricter enforcement of the vice laws was a post-war fact of life since the politicians knew it would take very little to inflame the anti-vice crusaders into action again. A man could still drink, and he could still gamble more or less openly, but finding a prostitute took more effort.

So Prohibition, coming less than three months after the partial loosening of restrictions following the end of World War I, and the reform movement that preceded it, must have seemed like the biblical plagues of Egypt to entertainment and vice operators in the Tenderloin and elsewhere in San Francisco. The Volstead Act, authorizing enforcement of the Eighteenth Amendment, was passed on October 28, 1918 and the United States became dry on January 17, 1919. While decades of reform and World War I restrictions never completely closed the lid on the Tenderloin, Prohibition did it overnight. The restaurants, cafes, and night spots, no matter how respectable, closed down because the public wouldn't go out for fancy dinners, shows, and dancing if the restaurants couldn't provide beer, wine, or liquor so people could loosen up and enjoy themselves.

Since there weren't any legal places to get drinks, other venues began to fill this vacuum. These were dance halls that took advantage of the Jazz Age coming into full bloom in the Roaring Twenties where young people smuggled in their own alcohol. Or else they went to speakeasies, many of which quickly opened in the Tenderloin, where customers could drink, eat, dance, and even catch a show, if they didn't mind the risk—relatively small in San Francisco—of a raid.

San Francisco didn't suffer as badly under Prohibition as many other cities. For one thing, organized crime never really got a foothold in San Francisco primarily because local protection racket operators, such as Pete McDonough, prevented outside competitors from getting established in the city. One story had Chicago mobster Al Capone flying into Mills Field (now San Francisco International Airport) to visit with a view to expanding his liquor business. Instead, his arrival was met by local officials who wouldn't even allow him to step off the plane.

Another reason San Francisco got off comparatively easy during Prohibition was because enforcement of the liquor laws was problematic. There existed little enthusiasm among the electorate or municipal officials for the task. This left enforcement to federal and state agencies, without much support from local government. For example, the San Francisco Board of Supervisors passed a resolution instructing the Chief of Police not to enforce any Prohibition laws. And when someone did get arrested, an unenthusiastic jury of their peers would be unlikely to convict. This led to incidents such as one in which San Francisco Mayor "Sunny Jim" Rolph arranged for each delegate to the 1920 National Democratic Convention at the Civic Auditorium (then still called by its original name, Exposition Hall) to be greeted at their hotel by an elegantly attired lady in a white dress, who presented each one with a bottle of bonded bourbon whiskey that was much appreciated by the out of town delegates who had been subsisting on hootch since early 1919.

Bonded liquor was more readily available in San Francisco than in many other places in the United States because West Coast rum runners didn't brew or distill their own stuff. Instead, they sent ships up to Vancouver where legitimate Canadian distributors loaded the steamers with cases of legal, brand-name liquors that were brought back down to the California coast, outside the three-mile limit, and run by speed boats into isolated coves, where the loads were convoyed to nearby towns and cities. Thus, the illegal brewing and distilling that attracted organized crime in other parts of the United States didn't take hold in San Francisco—except for some smalltime local operators. This resulted in fewer incidences of gang violence than in many other cities.

What little local enforcement remained was occasioned by Union Square businessmen in the early 1920s through a new district attorney who made several unsuccessful attempts to close down the cafes, the quasi-legal gambling clubs, the hotel prostitution rings, and the speakeasies that cropped up or remained after World War I. This was intended to clear the area for a westward expansion of the Union Square shopping district and to clean up the theater district. At the same time, two Methodist congregations built churches with dry hotels in the Tenderloin. There were also the occasional highly publicized raids by state and federal authorities. But every time they put a bootlegger out of business, another would take his place.

Union Square businessmen had been trying to chase vice out of the neighboring Tenderloin since the 1890s. The increasing respectability of the eastern edge of the district was accomplished through inroads along Powell Street with the Elkan Gunst Building on the northwest corner of Powell and Geary streets, and with the Bank of Italy (later the Bank of America) replacing the Techau Tavern with its new headquarters building on the northwest corner of Powell and Eddy streets (now the Forever 21 store and the Lofts at One Powell).

As for gambling, the late nineteenth and early twentieth century bookie joints and incorporated card clubs continued to operate in the Tenderloin. Before World War I, the district had been the place to go to organize and bet on horse races and boxing matches. After the war, men and women could still bet on a nag they fancied or a boxer they liked, though now they had to go to a bookie joint hidden in back of a storefront cigar stand instead of going to one of the openly run pool rooms that used to be concentrated in the southeast corner of the neighborhood. San Francisco historian Jerry Flamm wrote that some of the Tenderloin card clubs attracted the most accomplished gamblers in the country, men so famous that other players would pay to get in a game at a nearby table just to watch them. Other games were out and out against the law, roulette and craps being popular examples. These were busted on sight during raids, or if the operators weren't paying their dues.

The Tenderloin became one of the places to watch boxers train and to organize matches in places like Taussig & Ryan's storefront gym on Leavenworth Street in the Cadillac Hotel. And gamblers could still play in the card rooms, although the rooms' private club charters were merely a legal fiction under which they offered poker to the general public.

By and large, the old Tenderloin hotel district had been rebuilt by World War I. One of the effects of Prohibition was the replacement of restaurants that served alcohol by a network of cafeterias that didn't, like the Clinton, Compton, and Foster chains with multiple locations in the Tenderloin, and also the White Log Coffee Shops with their trademark white-painted *faux* log cabin exteriors. These became part of the infrastructure supporting the thousands of downtown workers who lived in Tenderloin and South of Market residential hotels.

The beginnings of the Tenderloin's Greektown were seen during this period. Greek-Americans moved from of their enclave around Third Street in the South of Market area and opened several grocery stores in the southeast section of the Tenderloin in the 1920s, followed by several social clubs in the same area in the 1930s.

The demand for small apartments for unmarried office workers increased with the continued growth of American cities' office-based economies. In San Francisco, an apartment building construction boom occurred after the closing of the Panama Pacific International Exposition at the end of 1915. These were mainly studio apartments in the still to be redeveloped west half of the Tenderloin and lower Nob Hill. William Murphy invented the Murphy In-A-Dor-Bed in San Francisco, which was designed specifically for these types of apartments, and he made a fortune with this and other foldaway features such as tables and ironing boards. While these apartments were often shared by young married couples or roommates, or were rented by bachelors, they were also sometimes called "mistress apartments" since they were likewise used by well-off men for housing young women during affairs.

More and more young entry-level office workers were out-of-town naïfs. This created a need for inexpensive housing that offered at least minimal guidance and protection. This took the form of a YMCA with rooms for young men on Golden Gate Avenue and Leavenworth Street in 1910, a Salvation Army Evangeline Residence for young women on McAllister Street in 1924, and a YMCA Hotel for young men on Turk Street in 1928 (that started admitting young women in 1934). These were the first examples of subsidized housing in the Tenderloin.

Though the size of the Tenderloin's floating and permanent population of entertainment industry workers in the 1920s was at first maintained and perhaps even augmented by the advent of the era of the huge palace movie theaters, advances in film technology making it possible to show extended length films began to have their effect. Even though films were typically accompanied by star turns and live vaudeville acts well into the 1940s, theaters started replacing live acts with movies as early as the 1920s. This, along with the rapid decline of vaudeville and hence the number of entertainment industry workers, was most visible when the venerable Orpheum Theater was demolished in 1938. During the Great Depression when people spent less money on entertainment, there was less demand for musicians and music. This caused the Musicians Union on Jones Street between Turk and Eddy (now a Christian elementary school) to begin losing members who moved south to find work with the growing movie industry in Los Angeles.

The Tenderloin also became the neighborhood with most of San Francisco's parking garages. These were built starting in 1906, with most constructed between World War I and World War II when automobile ownership became more common as larger numbers of people lived downtown or drove there to work, dine, drink, catch a show or a movie, and dance.

This was a period in which writers living in the Tenderloin began publishing their works with the neighborhood sometimes appearing as a character. This began in the 1920s with Dashiell Hammett's short stories about the Continental Op—the quintessentially nameless detective and antihero of American literature who someone once called the toughest man west of the Mississippi—and continued with Hammett's character Sam Spade in *The Maltese Falcon*. The Continental Op stories were written when Hammett was living in the Crawford Apartments on Eddy Street between Larkin and Polk (still extant).

Literary scholar Don Herron wrote that several other writers lived in the neighborhood, such as true crime, mystery, and science-fiction writer Miriam Allen DeFord, who lived and wrote in a two-room suite in the Ambassador Hotel on the corner of Mason and Eddy streets (still extant) from 1936 to just before her death in 1975. Herron also listed South African writer Alan Paton who completed his novel *Cry, the Beloved Country* while staying at the Hotel Somerton on Geary Street between Mason and Taylor in 1947 (now the Hotel Diva). Charles Willeford worked on his first novel, *The High Priest of California*, while living in the Hotel Powell near the cable car turntable in 1951 (now the Hotel Axiom). And, Fritz Lieber wrote *Our Lady of Darkness* while living in the Hotel Union on Geary Street between Hyde and Larkin (still extant) from late 1973 through 1975. Writers such as William Vollman are still doing this today. Marin County writer Court Haslett has written several neo-noir novels about a late 1970s Tenderloin resident named Sleeper Hayes and his adventures on its mean streets.

Brothels reappeared in the Tenderloin in the 1930s. These were high-end businesses run by madams like Sally Stanford and Dolly Fine, as well as many other, more pedestrian, operations.

Meanwhile, the neighborhood's prominence as a vice and crime district may have influenced a decision to move the old police station on Bush Street and Van Ness Avenue down the hill to the western edge of the Tenderloin in 1935, to Ellis between Polk Street and Van Ness Avenue (now the San Francisco Unified School District Student Nutrition Services office). There has been a police station in the district almost every year since.

But the city administration shot itself in the foot in 1935 when it hired former FBI agent Edwin N. Atherton to investigate charges of corruption in the San Francisco Police Department during a wave of civic indignation over this issue. Atherton wrote that he believed the majority of San Franciscans wanted an open city where vice was tolerated, and he hoped exposure of the corruption associated with the suppression of vice would accomplish this end. But he suspected the city intended to file-and-forget the resulting report, so, he made sure the newspapers reported his findings, which forced a grand jury investigation that resulted in the downfall of the long-standing McDonough brothers' protection racket. But the politicians, fearful of backlash from reformers and afraid of being implicated in the probe, used Atherton's report to launch an anti-vice crusade to distract attention from their complicity in the long-standing extortion scheme.

The crackdown didn't stop Tenderloin gambling, but it did push the brothels away from the Tenderloin onto the edge of Nob Hill. However, the heat stayed on, partly because of pressure on the city from large hotel owners to clean out the Tenderloin in preparation for the expected influx of tourists for the 1939 Golden Gate International Exposition on Treasure Island.

On March 22, 1933, the beginning of the end of Prohibition was announced when President Franklin D. Roosevelt, who had been elected partly on his promise to enact repeal, signed a law legalizing the manufacture and sale of 3.2% beer in the United States. The anti-Prohibition movement had been gaining strength as it became apparent the law didn't have the hoped-for effect of decreasing the impact of alcohol on the economics of the working classes. People drank anyway. Also, the alcohol industry and related agricultural jobs eliminated by Prohibition were needed to help inject money back into the economy and the government needed the lost tax revenues for the same reason.

One of the interesting, though unintended, effects of Prohibition was the appearance of homosexual speakeasies in urban areas because of the loosened behavioral constraints of the Roaring Twenties. Whether this trend included San Francisco is unclear. But by the time of Repeal, a number of cities around the world—New York and Berlin and Paris are examples—were known for their homosexual bars and cabarets. At least one or two of these opened in the Tenderloin as early as 1935, and what was apparently San Francisco's first bathhouse for homosexuals opened in 1938. During the 1920s and 1930s, Union Square was a well-known pickup spot. As a consequence, the police were likely tolerant of, or may even have encouraged, the existence these nearby bars simply to draw cruising activity away from Union Square and into these more discrete locations in the nearby Tenderloin.

But 1939 signaled the beginning of a return to greater prosperity for the district. The Golden Gate International Exposition brought more tourists to San Francisco and to the Tenderloin. Several new hotels were built in the neighborhood and a number of existing Tenderloin hotels were renovated to accommodate the increased demand for rooms. A mildly salacious guidebook, *Where to Sin in San Francisco*, was published in 1939. It was very popular, included a number of venues in the Tenderloin, and went into several editions over a 15-year period.

Moreover, reinstatement of the military draft and the beginning of American rearmament in 1940 continued this trend toward better times because a larger military meant more servicemen from the Bay Area's growing number of military bases visiting the Tenderloin's attractions, such as they were, and new armaments contracts meant more work for locals and more workers moving to the Bay Area, many of whom lived or sought recreation in the neighborhood.

Above: Eddy Graney, a former farrier and boxer, was a referee, a past and current owner of several Tenderloin cafes and billiard rooms, a politician, and president of a San Francisco boxing club. For years San Francisco's athletic clubs had been fighting amongst themselves for lucrative permits from the city to stage boxing matches. After the Union Labor Party came into power in 1906, political boss Abe Ruef suggested the clubs form an association and hire him—at a grossly inflated fee—as its representative to regularize the process of awarding permits. That is, permits would go only to members of the association. Graney was famous for originating the fashion in which boxing referees wore tuxedos. Here he is about to judge a contest between Jack Dempsey and Willie Meehan in 1918. [*William Walcott Collection*]

Opposite page: As one *San Francisco Chronicle* reporter wrote, "Clinton's owed its birth to Prohibition. Before the advent of the dry era, this basement corner of the Flood Building had been the Portola Louvre, a night club. But a night club needs more of a fiscal lubricant than plain ginger ale, so E. J. Clinton bought the lease"[1] in 1920 after he'd opened his first cafeteria on O'Farrell Street between Stockton and Powell (now Macy's) just four years before. The cafeterias attracted customers, especially locals who lived or worked in the neighborhood, by their fancy presentation: white tablecloths, silverware, and small orchestras. Downtown workers and residents became so attached to them that when the cafeterias started closing down in the 1950s it was a big enough deal for the newspapers to write full page feature stories about them. [*Glenn Koch Collection*]

Clinton's

CAFETERIA ★ 18 POWELL STREET
SAN FRANCISCO

Before ambient music systems became widespread, businesses that needed background music had to hire musicians. The Tenderloin, being a center of the city's night life, was also the center of its music industry. The Musicians Union was headquartered there and many of the city's music-related businesses were also there. Working musicians lived in Tenderloin hotels and apartments. Scenes like the one pictured above at Leighton's Cafeteria in the Douglas Building on the gore corner of Market and Eddy streets in the 1920s (now Hallidie Plaza) were common. [*Glenn Koch Collection*]

44 McAllister Street, San Francisco, Calif.

The Evangeline Residence was completed in 1923 as an inexpensive Salvation Army hotel for young women new to San Francisco. It was one of the Tenderloin's earliest subsidized housing projects and was staffed by a resident married couple who were Salvation Army officers. It offered a safe place to live for the tenants, most of whom had never lived in a city before. The Salvation Army sold the building to the Tenderloin Neighborhood Development Corporation about 1981, which operates it as a subsidized hotel for low income individuals. [*Glenn Koch Collection*]

According to biographer Kevin Cook, fabled gambler Titanic Thompson (whose real name was Alvin Thomas) was brought to San Francisco by Chicago gambler "Nick the Greek" Dandolos in 1924 to get into big time gambling. They played poker at the Kingston Club above Coffee Dan's on Powell and O'Farrell streets (now Skechers) where over a period of a year or two Thompson lined up suckers for large stakes golf games. [*Author's collection*]

Joe Parente was an Ellis Street tailor who went into the bootlegging business during Prohibition, buying four small steamships to sail to Vancouver, British Columbia to bring back shipments of bonded scotch, whiskey, gin, and whatever else would sell, which he purchased wholesale from a Canadian liquor company. [*San Francisco Examiner*]

One of Parente's ships, the *Quadra*, was seized by the Coast Guard in 1924 with a load of liquor worth $800,000. A treaty with Great Britain had extended the three-mile limit, within which a rum runner could be apprehended, out to twelve miles. This, and being low on fuel, made her captain risk getting too close to shore and she was boarded, seized, and towed to port. [*San Francisco Call*]

JAMES CLAY
DUNPHY

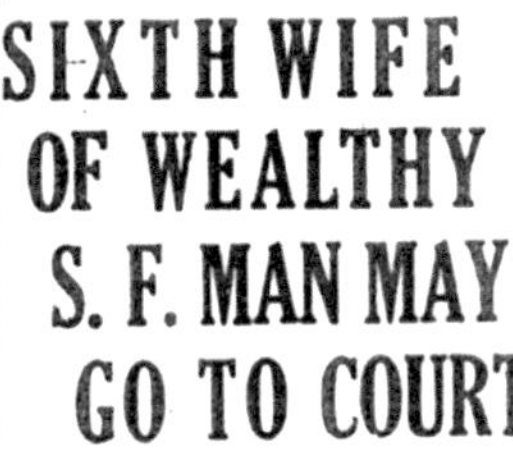

SIXTH WIFE OF WEALTHY S. F. MAN MAY GO TO COURT

Woman Separated From Millionaire Many Years Cut Off From Estate

Declares Herself Legal Heir and Feels She Is Entitled to Something

The troubles of James Clay ("Jimmie") Dunphy, millionaire of many marriages, follow him to the grave. Mrs. Anita Gannon Dunphy, his sixth wife, separated from him for years, came forward yesterday to meet the reading of his will with a threat to contest.

"I understand," said Mrs. Dunphy at her home, 1119 Webster street, yesterday, "that Jimmie left me entirely out of his will. I cannot submit to that, though I have had no time to consult a lawyer nor make up my mind what action to take. I feel, though, that I am entitled to something. I am his widow and his legal heir. He deserted me in life. He cannot desert me in death."

Half of Estate Left to His 70-Year-Old Sister

Dunphy's will, filed for probate in the Superior Court yesterday by Attorney Perry Evans, made no provision for his widow. The will provides that one-half of the estate, worth approximately $30,000, shall go to Mary D. Flood. Dunphy's

Estate Fight Links Names

James Dunphy, who grew up in St. Ann's Valley as the son of millionaire cattle baron William Dunphy and lived most of his adult life just two-and-a-half blocks away in the Hotel Herald on the northwest corner of Eddy and Jones streets, left a quarter of his supposed estate to a woman writer (bottom photograph) who also lived in the hotel with her mother. When still a young man he fell apart after the accidental death of his fiancé and spent the rest of his life going on binges and engaging in brief marriages to fortune-seekers who he would divorce after he sobered up. But despite years of rumors and newspaper reports about his fortune, it turned out he had achieved the not-so-elusive goal of many hard-living imbibers to spend it all before he died. He left just enough left to pay for his interment.

[*San Francisco Chronicle*]

Fischer's Dancing Pavilion, shown here in 1925 on the northeast corner of Eddy and Jones streets (now Boeddeker Park), was one of the hundreds of dance halls to spring up across the United States in the Roaring Twenties. These halls offered a solution to Prohibition: provide a dance hall and let the public BYOB—discreetly, of course. That's the Roosevelt Hotel being built across the street (now the Marlton Manor). [*shapingsanfrancisco*]

Glide Memorial Episcopal Methodist Church South, as it was named in its first San Francisco city directory listing, and its Methodist apartment-hotel next door were built with a million dollars from the Glide Foundation, which was set up by Lizzie Glide, a Southern Methodist from California's Central Valley who prayed for years for enough money to build a church in the Tenderloin. The discovery of oil on an otherwise worthless parcel of land inherited from her husband provided her with the funds to do it. Despite Prohibition, Methodist denominations felt it necessary to build combination church-hotels so that their congregants, who were dry, would have someplace to stay that didn't serve alcohol, legally or otherwise. Glide was a conservative organization until 1962, when the shrinking remains of the congregation, which was down to around thirty souls, forced the Glide Foundation to hire a new director to beef up membership or risk losing its tax-exempt status, since it had little to spend its money on from its income-earning investments. The new director, a Methodist preacher and former civil rights activist from the South named Rev. John Durham, hired younger pastors who outreached to homosexuals and seniors, focusing on social change and advocacy. Even though at that time both the Tenderloin and Glide's congregation were almost entirely white, they hired Rev. Cecil Williams as the church's first black pastor, and in the second half of the 1960s he shifted the church's focus from social change to social work and expanded the church's outreach to prostitutes, addicts, alcoholics, the disabled, and the poor in general. The apartment building next door was repurposed into offices for Glide's new programs. [*Western Neighborhoods Project/Emiliano Echeverria/Randolph Brandt Collection*]

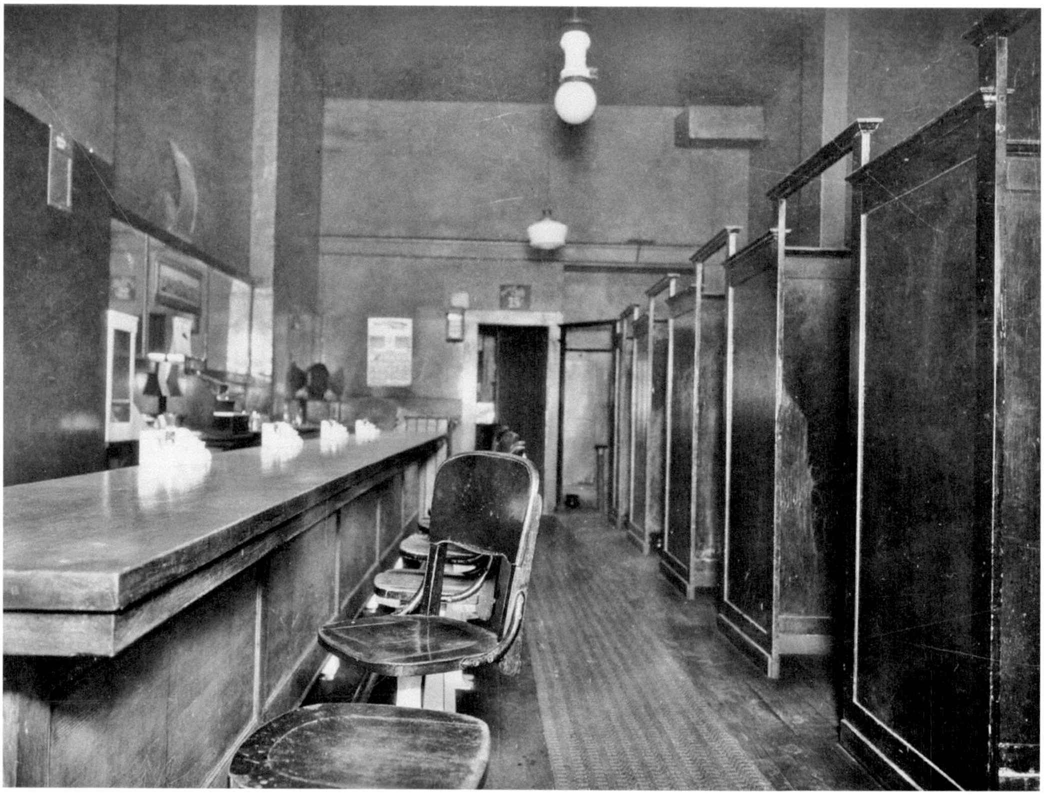

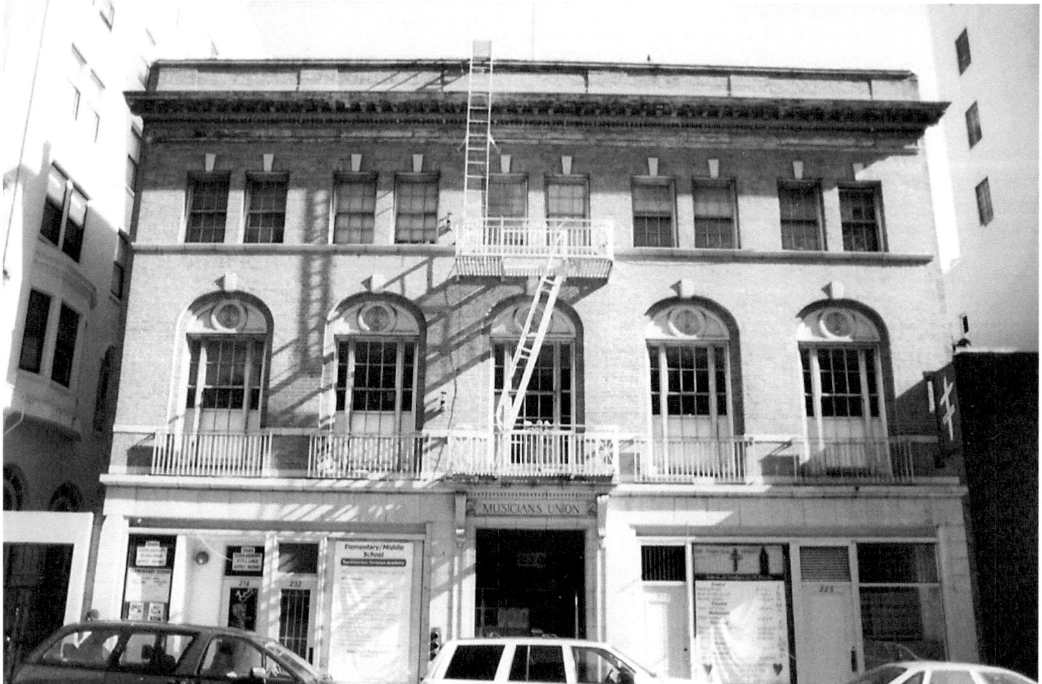
MUSICIANS UNION
Elementary/Middle School

Above: Bernstein's Fish Grotto began as Bernstein's Marine Grotto at 123 Powell Street between Ellis and O'Farrell (now a Uniqlo store) in 1917. According to a *San Francisco Chronicle* article, the iconic frontage, modeled after Cristoforo Colombo's ship *Niña*, was added in 1930. It was a Powell Street landmark until a particularly extortionate rent increase closed it in 1986. The Chauffeur's Club, one of the Tenderloin's gambling joints, operated for a time upstairs from Bernstein's. [*Author's collection*]

Opposite above: Harold McGuire's Crystal Sandwich Shop at 110 Eddy Street between Mason and Taylor in 1931 (now the Hotel Bijou), was one example of a downscale San Francisco speakeasy. According to the newspapers, one could get a beer and maybe even a drink as well as food. [*San Francisco History Center/San Francisco Public Library*]

Opposite below: The Musicians Union Hall was built about 1924 by architect Sylvain Schnaittacher on Jones Street between Turk and Eddy (now the San Francisco City Academy) in what is roughly the geographic center of the Tenderloin. For years there were separate black and white Musicians Union locals and there was an unwritten but rigidly enforced rule that blacks weren't permitted to work east of Van Ness, except for places in the Barbary Coast. In 1948, Barney Deasy opened Blanco's Cotton Club on O'Farrell Street (now the Great American Music Hall), patterning it after Harlem's Cotton Club with black waiters, black bartenders, black cooks, and a black band. But the Musicians Union told Deasy he couldn't do this because they didn't want blacks in the union. Deasy went ahead and opened anyway, the musicians crossed the union's picket line and in a couple of days the pickets went away. [*Author's collection*]

By the mid-1930s, a couple of clubs for homosexuals had opened in the Tenderloin. They were probably tolerated by the police in the hopes that they would draw cruising traffic away from where it was then centered in Union Square Park. The Kit Kat Club was in the basement of the Hotel Bristol on the southeast corner of Mason and Eddy streets in 1935. [*San Francisco Chronicle*]

The Music Box was launched around 1936 in the old Blanco's Hotel and Restaurant building (now the Great American Music Hall) and featured "sophisticated entertainment for sophisticated people," that is, performances by dancing women unencumbered by too much clothing. In 1939, the Music Box's management decided to dispense with the clothing altogether and booked feather dancer Sally Rand, who was also operating her Nude Ranch in the Gayway at the Golden Gate International Exposition on Treasure Island. But the Music Box couldn't follow up its success with Miss Rand and went bankrupt in June 1940. [*Author's Collection*]

Text of Atherton's Repor

STIRS CITY—Edwin N. Atherton, graft investigator, whose sensational report was made public yesterday.

Higherups Blocked Him, Sleuth Says

Rossi, Roche, Shumate and Quinn Assailed

Here is the complete text of the long awaited report on graft in San Francisco by Investigator Edwin N. Atherton as it was made public yesterday by Superior Judge George J. Steiger:

Duration and Cost Of Investigation

On November 21, 1935, I commenced an investigation into charges of graft in the San Francisco Police Department, pursuant to employment by you (District Attorney Matt C. Brady) and under authority of an ordinance enacted September 23, 1935, by the Board of Supervisors.

As you know, at the time of my employment, the firm of Atherton and Dunn was being organized and, shortly afterwards, the investigation was taken over by this firm.

This investigation continued actively for more than a year with no new lines of inquiry being undertaken after December 1, 1936. All activity has now been definitely terminated so we are submitting this as a final report on the case.

The total amount of money received by us for fees, salaries and expenses, including supplemental services performed up to and including January 31, 1937, is $60,660.84. A complete statement of disbursements, together with vouchers, is being submitted under separate cover.

Purpose of Report

In preparing this report, no attempt shall be made to review the investigation step by step as it would be an almost endless tion with the volume and extent of police graft, sum up the results of a concrete nature and make such other comments and observations as may seem pertinent and constructive

Objectives of the Investigation

Instructions given to us at the beginning of this case were to investigate the allegations of graft in the San Francisco Police Department and to develop as much in the way of facts and evidence as possible on this subject. We were permitted to outline our own procedure so we determined upon a three point program, as follows:

1—To ascertain whether there was a substantial foundation for the allegations against the department.

2—To purge the department of the maximum number of corrupt officers.

3—To prosecute such officers wherever possible.

The first objective was, of course, a fundamental one, with action on the other two largely contingent thereon, so it had to be determined first. In this regard it might be pointed out that there was apparently no specific, dependable data available on the volume and extent of the alleged corruption or on the identities of the sources and beneficiaries of such corruption, if any. There

IN CHARGE — Peter P. McDonough, who is characterized as a "directing head" of McDonough Brothers, the bail bond firm, Atherton calls the "fountainhead" of corruption."

Edwin N. Atherton was a former FBI agent who the city hired to investigate Police Department corruption. Bail bondsman Pete McDonough ran the protection racket that had preyed upon the San Francisco underworld since the 1890s and was paying off judges, court officials, and police officers. The resulting scandal and crackdown on vice resulted in McDonough being driven out of business when his bail bondsman's license was revoked in November 1937. [*San Francisco Examiner*]

Original Joe's was first listed on Taylor Street between Turk and Eddy in 1941, though longtime owner Tony Rodin and a partner operated it as a bar after they took it over in 1938 from a Southern fried chicken joint called the Carolina Pines. It became a neighborhood institution, and nearly everybody who was anybody at nearby City Hall ate there, as well as rock and roll stars on breaks from recording sessions at the nearby Wally Heider Studios. A fire shut down the Taylor Street restaurant in 2007. After insurance problems and the state of the neighborhood made it a poor business risk to resume operations, it became the last of the upscale old-time restaurants to leave the Tenderloin. It reopened in North Beach in 2012. [*Author's collection*]

Above: The owners of the otherwise respectable Hotel Somerton squeezed gambler Eddie Sahati for as much rent as they could get for letting him turn what used to be the ladies' bridge parlor into the Somerton Bridge Club, one of the Tenderloin's best-known poker rooms. This 1938 photograph is of the hotel's new Streamline Moderne marquee, which was installed in anticipation of the expected crowds of tourists for the Golden Gate International Exposition the following year. [*San Francisco History Center/ San Francisco Public Library*]

Opposite page: In 1939, the first edition the of a little volume titled *Where to Sin in San Francisco* was published, apparently directed towards tourists in anticipation of the second year of the Golden Gate International Exposition on Treasure Island. The text directed its readers to most of the major (and safe) restaurants, bars, clubs, and what-have-you in the city ... until the end of the volume, when it suddenly came down to earth and bluntly warned the reader off gambling games anywhere in San Francisco, especially in North Beach and the Tenderloin. "Within a half-mile of Jones and Turk, it's said, there are fifty places where you can lose every nickel you've got in less time than it took you to read this chapter."[2] [*Author's collection*]

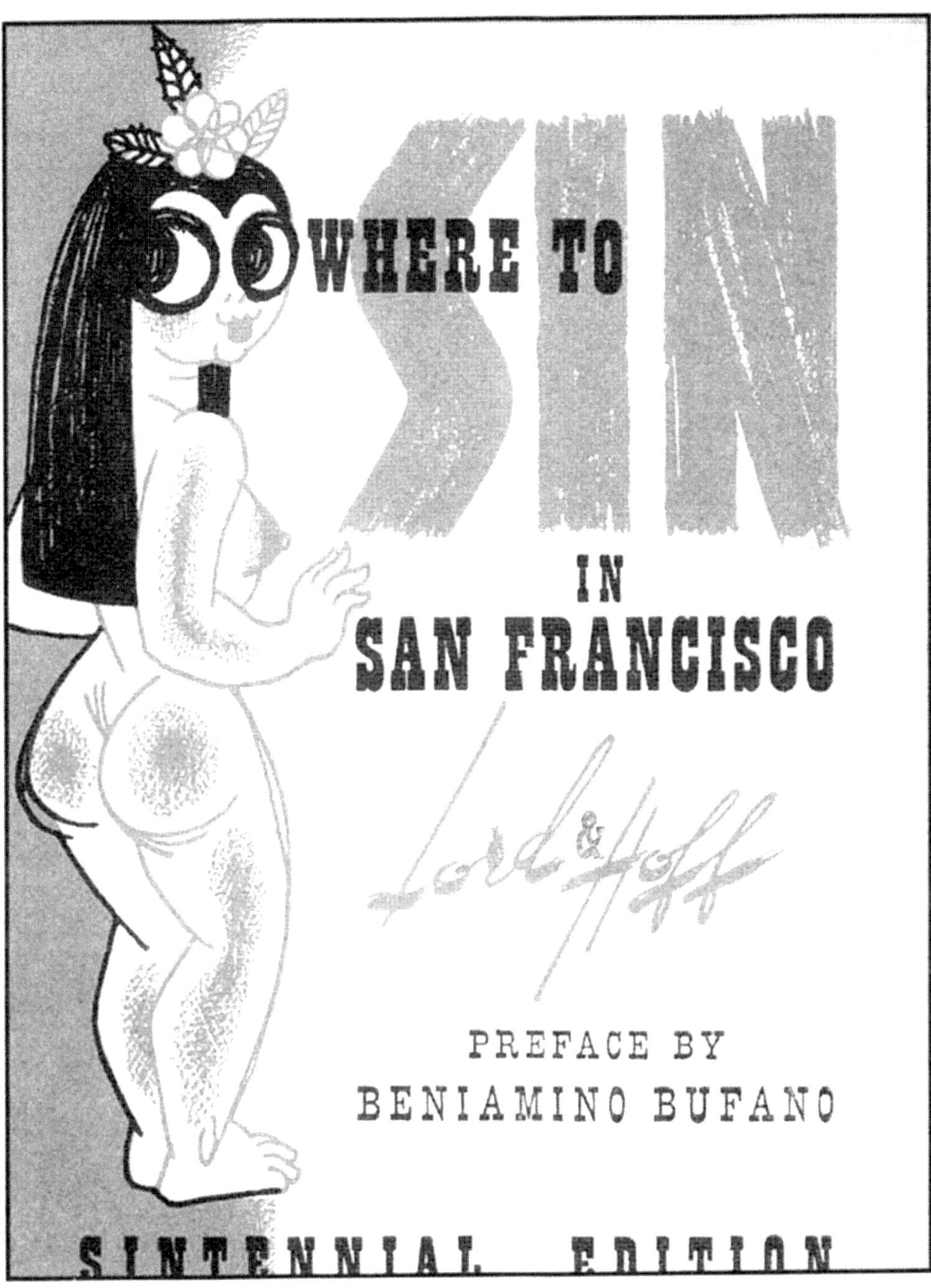

ENDNOTES

1. "Clinton's—a Dining Room Just Like Home—Closes Up," *San Francisco Chronicle*, December 24, 1950, 7.
2. Jack Lord and Lloyd Hoff *where to Sin in San Francisco* (San Francisco, Jorgenson & Co., 1939), 173.

FOUR

WORLD WAR II AND THE KOREAN WAR

World War II was a time of economic revival for the Tenderloin. The city's population grew precipitously with the influx of servicemen and war industry workers where three shifts meant the streets were filled day and night with people looking for a good time. And everyone had money to spend as the war years dropped unemployment to record lows. The big band tradition of the Roaring Twenties and the Great Depression continued to require large numbers of musicians, with clubs and dance halls paying top dollar for talent. True, entertainment costs had gotten high, but so had wages. And much of this new activity was in the Tenderloin.

In the 1940s, several Greek cafes opened in the southeast corner of the Tenderloin, joining the Greek-American social clubs and groceries that had transplanted themselves there in the 1920s and 1930s, and significantly enlarging the colony into a little Greektown.

NBC replaced its studios in the Hunter-Duhlin Building on Sutter Street by the construction of its much larger Radio City in 1942 at Taylor and O'Farrell streets, with its constant (at least at first) need for musicians, actors, actresses, announcers, and technicians. One of the benefits NBC brought to the neighborhood—the Musicians Union building was just three-and-a-half blocks down the hill—was a need for a full orchestra to be on duty and ready to play at a moment's notice eighteen hours a day in case of an unforeseen interruption of the performance or broadcast.

When World War II began, the military commenced periodic sweeps of bars and clubs for homosexual servicemen who would then be detained for a short time and discharged en masse from the service. Many of the men decided to stay in the cities where they were released instead of returning home to their families to try to explain their dishonorable discharges. The increase in the number of homosexual men in these cities, including San Francisco, resulted in an increase in the number of bars serving them. One historian wrote that by 1950 there were at least thirty-four such bars in San Francisco. Many of these were in the Tenderloin, which had the first of these venues in San Francisco in the mid-1930s. But in 1951 the California Supreme Court ruled that homosexuals have the right to assemble and so the number of bars in San Francisco catering to homosexuals began to increase, particularly in the Tenderloin, which also triggered greater efforts to suppress them.

Up until the end of World War II, San Francisco's major industries were transportation, shipping, and manufacturing. But after the war the economics of American urban centers began to change. The catastrophic loss of jobs as war industries shut down created rampant unemployment at the same time military veterans were returning home and looking for work. In addition, businesses began moving to the suburbs and the countryside, where labor was cheaper and more plentiful, and real estate costs were a fraction of what they were in the big urban areas. Many of the city residents who had these jobs followed them, while others moved elsewhere to find work. This caused San Francisco's population to shrink, the first major U.S. city in which this happened.

In 1944, the Tenderloin's one remaining public elementary school was moved elsewhere, a sign that families had abandoned the neighborhood. But the post-World War II baby boom apparently reversed this trend, for in 1951 the St. Boniface School resumed its city directory listing for the first time in decades. Meanwhile, San Franciscans found themselves having a harder time finding work among the kinds of jobs that were still available. Some couldn't easily adjust to the labor needs of a growing white-collar urban economy. Men and women who worked with their hands found it difficult to fit into an office job. Many of these workers lived in the Tenderloin. One sign of a growing unemployment problem was when St. Boniface Church found it necessary to open the St. Anthony Dining Room in 1950 on the southwest corner of Jones Street and Golden Gate Avenue, the Tenderloin's first soup kitchen since the Depression.

The entertainment industry, central to the Tenderloin's fiscal health for over half a century, also changed after the war. A growing taste for sentimental crooners by a public that was getting married and staying home to raise families meant there was less work for big bands and there was declining patronage of the large dance halls, clubs, and hotels that hired them. At the same time, musicians' wages remained high and the wartime entertainment tax continued after the war was over, making live entertainment expensive. Now people were going to smaller clubs with combos and a singer, so there was much less work in the Tenderloin entertainment industry than before. One of these clubs was the Black Hawk, which opened in 1949 with a house band, led by the brother of one of the owners. The band played nostalgic favorites like "The Italian Wedding Song" until 1950, when, by switching to jazz, it became the Tenderloin's last major music venue—and one of the first to book both black and white musicians east of Van Ness Avenue in contravention of a longstanding unwritten union rule against black musicians playing downtown.

Also, NBC Radio City's promise as a neighborhood employment hub proved to be illusory. Advances in transmission technology in 1940 just when construction started on the new building made it redundant to a recently built Los Angeles facility, with the result that most of its operations were transferred to LA while the rest of the now largely empty building was either leased to other radio stations or left unused. One of NBC's most popular programs that did stay local was *One Man's Family* because the writer, Carlton E. Morse, refused to move. But the greatly downsized station switched to recorded music as live big band shows disappeared.

Another Tenderloin entertainment industry that died off was the film exchanges. During the years of the Hollywood studio system, films were made of highly flammable and explosive cellulose nitrate and had to be locally stored in fireproof buildings with multiple vaults for distribution to theaters. The exchanges were usually owned by the studios whose films they handled. But in 1948 and 1949, a series of court decisions forced the studios to divest themselves of their theater chains, which until then were required to take whatever films the studios offered. This meant the now independently-owned theaters could bid for whatever new releases they wanted instead of getting stuck with several B pictures for every A picture they were assigned. But the exchanges' death knell came in 1949, when the invention of an inexpensive version of relatively fire proof cellulose acetate safety film began to replace more incendiary cellulose nitrate film stock.

These two developments, the rise of independently owned movie theaters and the invention of inexpensive safety film, eliminated the need for local storage since movie rentals could now be negotiated directly with the studios and they could be safely shipped long distances directly from geographically centralized distribution facilities to the theaters. By the early 1960s, there were no major film exchanges left in the Tenderloin. This loss was only partially ameliorated by the offices of several new family owned movie theater chains moving into the neighborhood, like the Levin, Nasser, and Naify organizations.

The late 1940s saw the end of organized gambling in San Francisco, which until then was another one of the Tenderloin's economic standbys. Former California Governor Edmund G. "Pat" Brown worked at the cigar stand that fronted his father's storefront card room on Fifth Street between Market and Mission in the early 1920s when he was a law student. Later, as a young attorney, he had helped his father incorporate a new cardroom on the northeast corner of Eddy and Taylor streets in the Tenderloin (now the construction site of a Tenderloin Neighborhood Development Corporation family housing project). He also drew up a charter for the Menlo Club, a card club on Turk Street between Mason and Taylor (now a private parking lot). Historian Jerry Flamm wrote that Brown soon found himself faced with several dilemmas. One of them was that he'd married the daughter of the captain of the Central Police District, which included the Tenderloin. Captain Layne had a record of coming down hard on gambling and for years Brown worried about the effects on his marriage, as well as on his political career, should his father be arrested by his father-in-law, or should the Menlo Club be raided and the issue of the club's charter come out.

When he ran for San Francisco District Attorney in 1939 against the incumbent, ostensibly reform DA Matthew Brady, his father was still operating his card club. Brown feared his opponent would raise this issue in the election, and he very gently asked his father to close the club, which his father did right then and there—only to open it again the next day. However, Brown lost that election without the issue ever coming up. He next ran unsuccessfully for California attorney general and found that one of the Tenderloin's biggest gambling and saloon operators had supported his opponent. Then he ran again for the San Francisco district attorney's office after his father had died. This time he won, and he went after the Tenderloin card clubs, which, given their questionable legality, was like shooting fish in a barrel.

Brown's campaign eliminated organized gambling in the Tenderloin as well as much of the hustling, con games, and other petty crime that came with it. It also ended one of the remaining post-war revenue sources for neighborhood businesses. According to San Francisco native Jacob Schurman, a descendant of one of the Tenderloin's big hotel owning families, his ancestors blamed Brown for their loss of income:

> Gaming, [his father] would point out, involves lots of cash moving around fast. If a casino was closed in one of the hotels, rents would likely never be as good for us (the hotels didn't run them, just rented the space to them) nor would there ever be the kind of loose change that casino crowds spread around on the streets of shiny entertainment districts. Everything would change fast.[1]

And it did. There were still some bookmakers operating, but they were closed down over the next several years. The hundreds of people who used to come to the Tenderloin to gamble, and who spent money while they were in the neighborhood, now stayed away. The main attraction was gone.

Although brothels had been mostly chased out of the Tenderloin, call girl rings sprang up in their place, especially during the two wars. In these operations, men were referred to prostitutes in their apartments or hotel rooms by calling a phone number. This was also when prostitution moved into the bars in the form of B-girls and strippers.

By then city planners in San Francisco (as well as in most other urban areas) were already responding to downtown businessmen's plans to build an office and tourist economy based on the increasingly dominant FIRE (finance, insurance, and real estate) industries on the embers of the previous standbys of manufacturing, shipping, and transportation. This was seen as early as 1948, when the city moved the Tenderloin's only statue, the Native Sons (or Admission Day) monument, from where it stood since 1897 at the intersection of Market, Turk, and Mason streets to Golden Gate Park. Until then, the district's streets were two-way thoroughfares, appropriate for a neighborhood that people drove to. But the relocation of the monument was accomplished as part of a larger project, which was the changing of the neighborhood's thoroughfares from their former two-way pattern to an entirely one-way pattern to facilitate the flow of traffic through the Tenderloin instead of to it. City planners saw the area becoming less and less of a destination and going more and more downhill and acted accordingly.

Since the late-nineteenth century there have been countless numbers of sex venues in the Tenderloin, but by far the longest-lived was Chez Paree. This club was first listed in the city directories in 1942 at 150 Mason between Eddy and Ellis (now the Hilton Parc 55 Hotel) where it stayed for about twenty-six years. The photograph shows the original location in 1964. The sign was originally made for The Barbary Coast club in the International Settlement on Pacific Avenue. When that venue closed, Chez Paree's management acquired and repurposed it, as seen above. [*Courtesy of Alan L. Canterbury/San Francisco History Center/San Francisco Public Library*]

After moving to two other sites in the 1980s and 1990s across the street from the original storefront, Chez Paree's fourth and final location was two blocks west on Jones Street between Turk and Eddy in Terrance Alan's notorious building between 2004 and 2007, but without its famous leg sign. Maybe it was a sign of bad luck, for this time it closed down for good after a total run of 65 years in the Tenderloin. [*Author's collection*]

By 1959 this small triangular two-story building at 34 Jones Street between Market and Golden Gate was the Little India restaurant, two or three decades before the "Tandoor-loin" District was named for the Indian restaurants that clustered in the late 1980s on the blocks around O'Farrell and Leavenworth streets. Why was there an Indian restaurant in the Tenderloin as early as 1959? One likely reason was a new customer base: the city directory listed twenty-one people whose last names were Patel, and twenty of them were listed as owning or managing hotels. Though just one of these was located in the Tenderloin, another eighteen were located in the South of Market District, just across Market Street from the restaurant. [*Western Neighborhoods Project/Private collector*]

Elmer "Bones" Remmer was a leading Tenderloin cardroom and bar owner in the mid-1940s to mid-1950s. He was investigated by San Francisco District Attorney Edmund G. "Pat" Brown after World War II for running a gambling business while claiming it was a private club for members only, resulting in the shutting down of the Tenderloin card clubs. It was not lost on the press that Remmer had supported Brown's Republican opponent in a previous race for the California Attorney General spot, and that Tenderloin gambling club owners had supported longtime District Attorney Matt Brady when Brown ran against him and lost in 1939. [*Bancroft Library*]

The second floor of the building just to the right of the Hotel Dalt sign on Turk Street between Mason and Taylor (now a private parking lot) was a Tenderloin card room in 1915 called the Union Athletic Club. Tenderloin gambling and prostitution operator Jerome Bassity moved his Thirty-third Assembly District Club there in 1920. Joe Schreiber opened the Menlo Club there in 1930 and Bones Remmer bought it in 1945, the year this photograph was taken. [*San Francisco Chronicle*]

'You Can Count 'Em On Your Fingers'

A Sign is all that remains of the Golden Peacock restaurant on Eddy Street.

The Golden Peacock was one of the later Greek restaurants to open in the Tenderloin (first listed in the City Directory in 1968) after the surge of interest in Greek culture caused by the movies *Never on Sunday* in 1960 and *Zorba The Greek* in 1964. Moving from their original neighborhood around Third and Folsom, Greeks started opening grocery stores in the Tenderloin in 1920, followed by social clubs in the 1930s, and cafes and restaurants in the 1940s. The socioeconomic problems of the neighborhood in the 1970s adversely affected Greek businesses, and by the early 1980s there was little left of what had once been a small but thriving Greektown around Eddy and Mason streets. [*Central City Hospitality House/Tenderloin Times*]

Jazz singer Billie Holiday was arrested by federal narcotics agents at the Mark Twain Hotel on Taylor Street between Ellis and O'Farrell in 1949 where she and her manager-husband John Levy were staying during a gig in the city. The agents found a small amount of opium and a pipe in their room and Holiday was hauled down to the police station to be booked. [*Bancroft Library*]

By the end of the 1940s, the Tenderloin was falling on hard times again. World War II was long over, there were far fewer servicemen looking for action, and San Franciscans were getting older and staying home with their families. In this 1949 photograph of the northwest corner of Turk and Taylor streets, Mindy's had closed, and up Turk Street the banners for the Turk Club and the Blue & Gold looked old and worn. [*shapingsanfrancisco*]

The Grand Hotel on the southwest corner of Turk and Taylor (now the New Grand Apartments) was also owned by the Wilson family (just a block west of their Hotel Bristol). Like most of the family's edifices, it was designed by architect C. A. Meussdorfer. This hotel was opened on August 8, 1907. With the card clubs closed, less work for musicians, no more live variety theater, the first run movies moving away from Market Street to other neighborhoods, fewer servicemen, and other problems, the Wilson family and other property owners were already complaining about the area's economic decline. [*Jacob Schurman*]

The Black Hawk was the last major union musician venue in the Tenderloin. Most of the jazz greats of the era performed there, and it was one of the first places to allow black musicians to work east of Van Ness Avenue. It was just another cocktail lounge until 1950 when they booked then unknown Dave Brubeck. In a couple of weeks people started coming in to see him because a local radio station was talking about him, and it decided the owners to start booking jazz combos. In this 1961 photograph, Cal Tjader, George Shearing, and Andre Previn are advertised. [*San Francisco History Center/San Francisco Public Library*]

ENDNOTES

1. E-mail from Jacob Schurman to Peter Field, February 18, 2017.

FIVE

THE TENDERLOIN IN POST-WAR SAN FRANCISCO

Economic and social trends in America's post-war eras had a critical impact on the Tenderloin. The transition to a peacetime economy after World War II and again after the Korean War had a decidedly negative effect on the neighborhood's entertainment-based economy as the numbers of soldiers and sailors seeking entertainment shrank, the war industry workers vanished, and the remaining businesses went back to single shifts. Shortly after the end of the Korean War, the *San Francisco Chronicle* exposed the call-girl and B-girl rackets, as well as protection and extortion schemes run by the police, politicians, and some out-and-out swindlers who were preying on San Francisco bars, especially in the Tenderloin.

Like many heterosexual bars, a number of homosexual bars were run by shady characters and served rotgut booze, making them easy targets for extortion by crooked cops. The extortion stopped after the police investigated and prosecuted the coercion. In particular, the newspapers publicized what they called the gayola scandal. By this time there were enough homosexual bars in the Tenderloin and elsewhere for the newly formed Mattachine Society to publish and distribute a guide. Following the extortion scandal, the police increased crackdowns on homosexual bars until the courts ruled they could request revocation of an alcohol license only if they observed illegal activity. In spite of the raids, the number of these bars grew to fifty by 1955, and fifty-three by 1960. While the number of closings reached twenty-five, by 1962 another twenty-four had opened, most of them owned by the previous owners who obtained new liquor licenses through fronts. Also helping was the formation of the Tavern Guild in 1962, composed of homosexual bar owners and workers who helped fight off police crackdowns and generally supported its member bars.

Much of the police activity against Tenderloin bars may have been motivated by civic leaders eager to clean out the Tenderloin to pave the way for massive redevelopment projects such as the Downtown Center Garage and Conrad Hilton's hotel project next to a new downtown airline bus terminal, although at least one mayor had personal reasons for campaigning to clean up the area, having lost a brother to the seamier side of the neighborhood.

Many historians place the beginning of major losses of affordable residential hotel housing in the Tenderloin in the late 1970s, when the conversion of a number of residential hotels into tourist hotels began. But its real start was over twenty-five years earlier in the period between 1951 and 1968, when eleven large development projects were completed.

These started with the Department Store Center Building on O'Farrell Street in 1951, the Downtown Center Garage at Mason and O'Farrell streets in 1954, a parking lot at Turk and Taylor streets in 1956, the State Office Building on Golden Gate Avenue between Larkin and Polk in 1957, and the Downtown Airlines Bus Terminal in 1959. The six other projects were the New Federal Building; the Hilton Hotel; the Mosser Towers on Turk and Eddy streets between Leavenworth and Hyde; a PG&E substation at Larkin and Eddy streets, completed around 1963 or 1964; the enlargement of a parking lot on Eddy and Taylor streets in 1966; and the building of Hastings College of Law classrooms in 1968.

A major consequence of these projects was the demolition of at least twenty-eight inexpensive residential hotels and three apartment buildings. This initial wave of post-war redevelopment was the first of several, each of which resulted in further large losses of affordable housing in the Tenderloin. Beginning in the 1980s these losses were one of the causes of the homeless crisis because the number of affordable housing units had shrunk to the point that competition for tenants was eliminated and the rents on rooms in the remaining hotels kept increasing. Eventually a tipping point was reached where the rents were beyond what some people could afford for a room for a month. These people became homeless and as the inflation of residential hotel rents continued, so did the number of homeless grow.

However, few people (except public and private urban planners) in the 1950s and 1960s saw this as a problem or anticipated the long-term effects. Though it wasn't widely known until the 1960 census, San Francisco's population had begun to decline after the Korean War and one of the affected neighborhoods was the Tenderloin. Suddenly hotel owners couldn't get enough tenants and as this went on, many of the hotels stopped making money and were then sold, or were put on deferred maintenance, or were abandoned, or were demolished to make way for more profitable enterprises with low overheads such as street level open-air parking lots. Hardly anyone foresaw the inflation of the 1970s and the resumption of population growth in the 1980s that would make the loss of these hotel rooms a major urban housing crisis.

But in the 1950s and 1960s these projects represented to most people what amounted to the Tenderloin's first wave of economic redevelopment since the war years. Apparently, it was thought the rapidly dwindling numbers of servicemen and war industry workers would be replaced by hundreds or even thousands of people coming to the neighborhood every day to work, shop, eat, and find entertainment. An example of the optimism this development created was seen when Bank of America opened two neighborhood branches, one on Hyde Street and Golden Gate Avenue in 1960 (now an abandoned post office), and another on Ellis Street between Mason and Taylor in 1963 (now a small, dilapidated office building).

Another bright spot that occurred in the early 1960s was was the wave of interest in Greek culture was spawned by the movies *Never on Sunday* in 1960 and *Zorba The Greek* in 1964. This, along with some favorable restaurant reviews, contributed to a large uptick in business in the Tenderloin's Greektown area around Eddy and Mason streets. A less dazzling but equally profitable development was the pornographic bookstores, movie theaters, and massage parlors that began infesting the neighborhood in the early 1960s, catering largely to out-of-towners staying at the new Hilton, as well as to locals. Property owners with chronically vacant storefronts, even those who would have preferred more respectable tenants, started renting to less socially desirable businesses. A 1977 exposé by the *San Francisco Examiner* of conditions in the Tenderloin pointed out that local businesses, including sex venues, did as well or as badly as the Hilton was doing, mostly because of the number of customers the hotel brought into the area. But by the 1980s, the Greek businesses and the bank branches were going or gone as rising levels of homelessness and street crime drove out the area's remaining customer base.

Another blow to the Tenderloin's prosperity began earlier when downtown movie theaters lost their ability to attract crowds. For decades, new movies would open in the Market Street movie theaters and would only go to the outlying neighborhood theaters after their Market Street runs. The major Hollywood studios' divestiture of their theater chains detailed in chapter four meant that starting in the early 1950s, first-run movies began opening in neighborhood theaters as well in as the Market Street movie palaces. Theater historian Jack Tillmany wrote that this started the gradual dimming of Market Street's luster over the next forty years, as increasing movie rental costs and decreasing patronage resulted in the closing of one Market Street movie palace after another. The resulting loss of moviegoers and their spillover into Tenderloin restaurants and bars helped many neighborhood eateries and watering holes go out of business or move elsewhere.

Another economic misfortune was the loss of the Black Hawk jazz club, one of the last live downtown music venues still providing work for union musicians and bringing business to the Tenderloin. It started losing customers to television, rock and roll, and better-quality home sound systems in the late 1950s, and closed in 1963.

Yet another economic loss was the closing of Tenderloin chain cafeteria outlets in the 1950s and 1960s. These businesses depended on three groups of customers: entertainers and entertainment industry workers; neighborhood and downtown office workers, many of who lived in residential hotels and studio apartments in the Tenderloin; and a growing population of retirees of limited means, who also lived in Tenderloin SROs. As the first two customer bases shrank in size over these two decades—driven out by the loss of work and deteriorating conditions in the neighborhood—the remaining customer base proved to be inadequate to sustain the cafeterias. Just one, Manning's on Geary Street, held out until the 1980s.

Still another economic calamity was when Market Street was torn up in the early 1970s to build the Bay Area Rapid Transit system in San Francisco. The resultant disruption in traffic and transportation patterns caused many Market Street and Tenderloin businesses to lose customers to the point that they closed or moved elsewhere.

Most reports of Tenderloin street crime agree that the neighborhood was relatively safe as late as the end of the 1960s, and that street crime became more noticeable in the early 1970s. This was around the same time that residential displacement caused by urban renewal and gentrification in other neighborhoods like South of Market funnelled more vulnerable populations into the Tenderloin while increasing numbers of predators were also concentrated there for the same reasons. Basically, redevelopment decreased the number of neighborhoods where offenders on probation or parole could find cheap housing, or drug addicts and alcoholics could afford to live, causing more and more of them to end up in the Tenderloin, where they victimized the increasing numbers of seniors, disabled, and runaways who also ended up there. One result was that as the eastern half of the Tenderloin became less safe, underage male prostitutes and other sexual hustlers from the "meat rack" area around Mason Street were pushed west towards the legitimate homosexual bar scene on Polk Street. This, in turn, drove middle-class homosexuals from the Polk Street area into the Castro District.

The 1970s was also when the demographic composition of the neighborhood began to change. While the Tenderloin was almost entirely white up through the 1960s, during World War II it also became largely adult. Children then began to reappear in the Tenderloin after the war, enough of them for the St. Boniface School on Golden Gate Avenue between Jones and Leavenworth streets to resume its listing in the city directories in 1951 for the first time since the 1906 earthquake and fire—and just six years after the closing of the Adam's elementary school on Eddy Street between Polk and Van Ness. Starting in the very early 1970s, blacks moved into the southeast and south-central part of the Tenderloin, and by the 1980s, many of them were single mothers with their children. Starting in the mid- and late-1970s, Southeast Asian singles and families moved into the central and western areas. Latino families began moving into the area by the end of the decade. By the 1980s there were at least a thousand, and perhaps as many as three thousand, children.

Another demographic change was caused by the development of psychiatric drugs in the late 1950s and 1960s to treat major mental illnesses. This resulted in the discharges from state hospitals of large numbers of psychiatrically disabled individuals unable to care for themselves and needing maximum and immediate community support—much of which was never forthcoming. Frequently their only source of income was the federal Aid to the Totally Disabled program and this and the shortage of adequate community programs limited their housing options to rooming houses and cheap city hotel rooms. Urban renewal and neighborhood gentrification gradually eliminated these sources of housing in all but inner-city districts, concentrating these unfortunates in these districts—including in San Francisco's Tenderloin. Also funneled into the inner cities were the physically and medically disabled.

Towards the end of the 1970s, a wave of post-Vietnam War economic redevelopment began in the Tenderloin. Southeast Asian refugees who had moved to the Tenderloin began opening businesses around the same time that residential hotels in the eastern edge of the Tenderloin started converting to tourist hotels. Also at this time, several major tourist hotel projects were launched in the same area, connecting the 1960s development of the San Francisco Hilton more solidly with the Union Square tourist district.

Another wave of development was generally not acknowledged as such. This was the rise of service agencies in the neighborhood, which first appeared in a limited way in the early 1950s through the 1960s, and then grew steadily in the following decades.

Many observers think of service agencies as contributing to the problems of a community like the Tenderloin because they see them as magnets for the disadvantaged with resultant deleterious effects on the area. However, since service agencies tend to go where their clients are already living, and not the other way around, what this really means is that they make it easier for their clients to survive where they are already located. What attracts the poor and disadvantaged to neighborhoods is cheap rent and food. This is not to say that this population doesn't bring economic and behavioral problems with them, but it is other amenities besides service agencies that attract the poor to a neighborhood.

Moreover, social service agencies grew into one of the largest economic redevelopment forces in this district. They brought in hundreds of employees every weekday with money to spend in the neighborhood. As just one example, many Tenderloin restaurants came to depend at least in part on these employees as a steady supply of customers. In addition, these programs were a shot in the arm to Tenderloin real estate values in two ways: they were willing to rent and lease office space in areas that most businesses avoided, and over the years they bought up and rehabilitated many deteriorated buildings in the neighborhood. Taken as a whole, they became the second-largest group of property owners in the area, after private hotel owners, and now account for about a third of all the hotels in the Tenderloin.

Many, if not most of these construction efforts resulted in buildings of such quality that this alone contributed to increasing property values, as well as the business opportunities they provided through new storefront and office spaces, even though they housed the poor and disabled. In addition, street activity tended to move elsewhere after one of these projects was up and running. Because agency building owners usually wouldn't rent to liquor stores, legal and quasilegal sex outlets, and other socially marginal though highly profitable businesses, they contributed to an overall improvement of the neighborhood. As a matter of record, many building rehabilitations or new building projects resulted in the eviction of these less-desirable businesses. Over the years, one result was a substantial decrease in the numbers of socially negative enterprises in the area.

The neighborhood had been politically influential from the 1860s on, mostly under the Republican banner. But Democrat Edmund G. "Pat" Brown's war on gambling in the district when he was the San Francisco District Attorney in the late 1940s and early 1950s eliminated this last vestige of political influence from the neighborhood, which at that time consisted of card club owners who were contributing heavily to local and state political campaign coffers.

This helped shift political influence outside the district to downtown business and political interests. This was first seen in the large development projects of the 1950s and 1960s that tore down many aging residential hotels. The shift left the district without a political voice for about a decade-and-a-half until Glide Church emerged in the mid-1960s as a Tenderloin champion of two issues: demanding the designation of the Tenderloin as a fifth Economic Opportunity Council area to make it eligible for federal War on Poverty grants and advocating for homosexual rights.

At least one community organizer left the Tenderloin in the early 1970s, saying that the neighborhood had no social structure of its own and was impossible to organize. However, as Anthony Robinson wrote in *Community Mobilization and Regime Transformation in San Francisco's Tenderloin*, the failures of the decade of the "War on Poverty" of the mid-1960s to the mid-1970s had one positive result. It left behind a group of trained community organizers who saw their job as organizing poor neighborhoods in order to extract benefits such as law enforcement, development funds, housing, infrastructure improvement, and programs from the municipalities that had selectively ignored them since the Korean War. Some of these community organizers wound up in the Tenderloin in the late 1970s, and in 1980 the North of Market Planning Coalition opened an office on Eddy and Jones streets with a staff composed largely of VISTA volunteers supervised by several paid employees whose research and advocacy helped resurrect a more neighborhood-wide political voice than had been heard since the reform era before World War I. Another major contribution to the development of this voice was when Central City Hospitality House, one of the earlier programs to open in the district, started up a neighborhood newspaper, the *Tenderloin Times*.

At this point the district was caught in the same conundrum that most inner cities faced: how to clean up and make poverty areas habitable without pushing up property values and rents through unrestrained development that would drive out the people the improvements were supposed to benefit. The Tenderloin groups decided to compromise: stop big development projects from entering the neighborhood, make those they couldn't stop pay for the privilege with substantial mitigations, and encourage local small-scale development to improve the district's economy.

Essentially, community groups stopped further big developments in the mid-1980s by getting the neighborhood down-zoned to mostly residential and small business, and by successfully challenging several major development projects at the Planning Commission level. This slowed the conversion of residential hotels to tourist hotels by the passage of a city ordinance and provided legal representation to the affected tenants. It also forced big development projects, ones that were too far along to stop, to fund programs to mitigate the effects of the larger projects on the neighborhood. These organizers were also successful in getting four neighborhood parks for the growing number of children living in the Tenderloin and developing affordable housing projects of their own. (The creation of subsidized housing in the Tenderloin started in the late 1970s and has continued at a more or less steady pace ever since. As funding sources changed, the emphasis shifted from rehabilitation to new construction.) But community groups were only partially successful at preserving existing cheap residential housing from conversion into tourist hotels, and still less successful in trying to eradicate street crime and its causes.

Perhaps the most insurmountable obstacles to cleaning up the Tenderloin and developing small businesses were the emergence of homeless street people in the early 1980s, the continued placement of parolees and probationers in the area, and the failure of law enforcement to stop drug dealing or to control disruptive behavior on the streets. Starting with just a few dozen people in 1982, the number of homeless in San Francisco stabilized over the last several years at between seven and eight thousand individuals, with by far the largest number in the Tenderloin.

The presence of large numbers of predators fueled a serious neighborhood crime problem. One report in the 1980s found that Tenderloin hotels that were part of the homeless Hotline Hotel program had ninety-two percent more major crime reports than hotels that didn't accept clients from the program. According to another report, at one time the Hotline Hotel program was renting rooms in thirty-one hotels, most of them in the Tenderloin. One result was to increase the number of transients and decrease the number of permanent residents in these hotels.

In addition, by the end of the 1980s the rising street-crime rate, and the increase in problems caused by the behavior of street people and criminals, created a split between those in the neighborhood who wanted to clean things up, and those who wanted to protect civil rights. Many pointed the finger at this split as the main factor preventing any solution to these problems. But the real causes were more fundamental and outside the neighborhood: the economic forces discussed earlier were keeping people homeless and on the street, and the legal system no longer had the space or resources or even the mandates to adequately contain offenders or control disruptive behavior.

These factors increasingly drove off what remained of the Tenderloin's customer bases, and also kept many potential new customers from venturing into the neighborhood and supporting Tenderloin small businesses. The number of urban pioneers who were intrepid enough to explore neighborhoods like the Tenderloin weren't enough to sustain it economically.

In the 1990s, the Mid-Market, Tenderloin, and South of Market districts were becoming ripe for change. This had already started in a big way in the South of Market area—a long decaying former industrial district in which high-end private housing developments were being built at a rapid pace—initiating a radical change in the neighborhood's demographics, as well as its character. But politics kept this from spreading to the mid-Market/Tenderloin areas. In fairness, the politicians preventing this were attempting to protect the neighborhood from the effects of rising housing costs on Tenderloin residents.

But the social media era freed a long-stalled Mid-Market development plan at the end of the 2010s, which gave birth to the Twitter tax break, and finally loosed the forces of increasing real estate and rental costs on the Mid-Market corridor, which started a rush of upscale bars, restaurants, galleries, boutiques, and the like in the Tenderloin, to say nothing of its effects on the value of commercial real estate. Because the neighborhood had remained relatively undeveloped with respect to the rest of the city, it still had the most affordable downtown real estate for small business startups.

But now, neighborhood advocacy groups had become increasingly dormant, and the Central City Extra, which replaced the *Tenderloin Times* as a neighborhood voice after that latter paper folded, itself now folded, resulting in another lessening of neighborhood political influence, though some strong individual voices remained. The politicians were back in charge, and there was little effective opposition to the Mid-Market project and its effects on the Tenderloin. The resulting inflation in real estate values drove a number of rent-paying nonprofit service providers out of the Tenderloin, and in some cases out of San Francisco. It also pushed out many of the Southeast Asians who settled in the west half of Tenderloin the 1970s and 1980s, because they could no longer afford the rising rents.

In 1953, the Blue & Gold bar opened at 138 Turk Street between Taylor and Jones, an early sports bar celebrating the school colors of Cal Berkeley just across the Bay. It was a transvestite bar from the 1960s to the 1990s. By the 2000s the bar had become the City Impact Rescue Mission and the Boston Hotel. [*Author's collection*]

This Leavenworth Street building had been an Atherton Report site in 1937, meaning it housed a brothel. The soda fountain in the storefront was first listed in the city directories in 1953 but was really a front for a call-girl operation that was busted the following year. (Note the President Follies poster on the building next door.) It was the C & B Cafe in 1993, which was a front for the headquarters of a Chinese-Vietnamese gang that was into extortion, gambling, prostitution, smuggling immigrants, and car theft until it was raided that year. In 2002 it was the Cafe Thúy Hằng, known locally as the Cafe Thug Hang, and was raided four times in 2002 and 2003 for selling drugs and receiving stolen goods. It is now a legitimate Vietnamese business. [*San Francisco History Center/San Francisco Public Library*]

Photo: Phil Head

Jackson reflects on the changes he's seen in the Tenderloin during almost four decades working at the corner of Mason and Turk streets..

"Jackson," as he was known to all according to a *Tenderloin Times* interviewer, set up his shoeshine stand near the corner of Mason and Turk streets in 1954, and watched the neighborhood change over the next thirty-six years. He said people used to dress up in those days, they cared about their appearance, and of course would get their shoes shined. In 1990, when this photograph was taken, he described how much the neighborhood had deteriorated from a classy nighttime entertainment district when:

> There were always more people out at night than you'd see all day long ... You could walk on the streets any time, day or night, with a thousand dollars in your pocket, and nobody would touch you ... there were all kinds of classy restaurants in the Tenderloin in those days. And nice theaters like the Golden Gate... where you could see good movies and song and dance shows. Not all this porn stuff ...You could get a good room, and I mean a *nice* room for $30 a month.

But now, he says, "Go ring the bell and the roaches will open the door for you."[1] [*Central City Hospitality House/Tenderloin Times*]

McDonald's Books on Turk Street between Mason and Taylor was a neighborhood standby from 1954 until it closed in 2009. Conditions like that seen in this 2002 photograph drove away most of its business after the 1980s. [*Author's collection*]

Above: The Hotel Del Rey was demolished in 1955, when this photograph was taken, to clear the site for the Downtown Airlines Bus Terminal. But of special interest was the little white doorway on the Taylor Street side of the building with the swan-neck pediment above the door. According to Randy Shaw in his book *The Tenderloin: Sex, Crime and Resistance in the Heart of San Francisco*, this was the entrance to the 356 Club, a gay bar identified only by the numbers above the doorway. [*San Francisco History Center/San Francisco Public Library*]

Opposite above: In 1955, businesses like Romarco's at 162 Turk Street between Taylor and Jones (now the Helen Hotel) were still opening in the Tenderloin in the hopes that early signs of redevelopment meant a return of customers to the neighborhood. But it closed within a year or two. The crowds just didn't come. [*Bancroft Library*]

Opposite below: The Daughters of Bilitis was the first lesbian civil rights organization in the United States. Started in 1955 and meeting in participant's homes, they were recruiting and publishing a newsletter, *The Ladder*, by the following year. Their first city directory listing was in 1958 in an office next door to the Mattachine Society on Mission Street. They had an office the same year in the Department Store Center Building on O'Farrell Street between Stockton and Powell. [*Author's collection*]

THE LADDER

Monthly magazine of articles, stories, poems, book reviews, quotes, comment and significant opinion on sexual problems facing the Lesbian in society today. Published by The DAUGHTERS OF BILITIS, Inc., non-profit educational, research and social service organization. Subscriptions mailed in sealed plain envelope, $2.50.

DAUGHTERS OF BILITIS

165 O'Farrell Street, Suite 405 San Francisco 2, Calif.

Telephone YUkon 2-9290

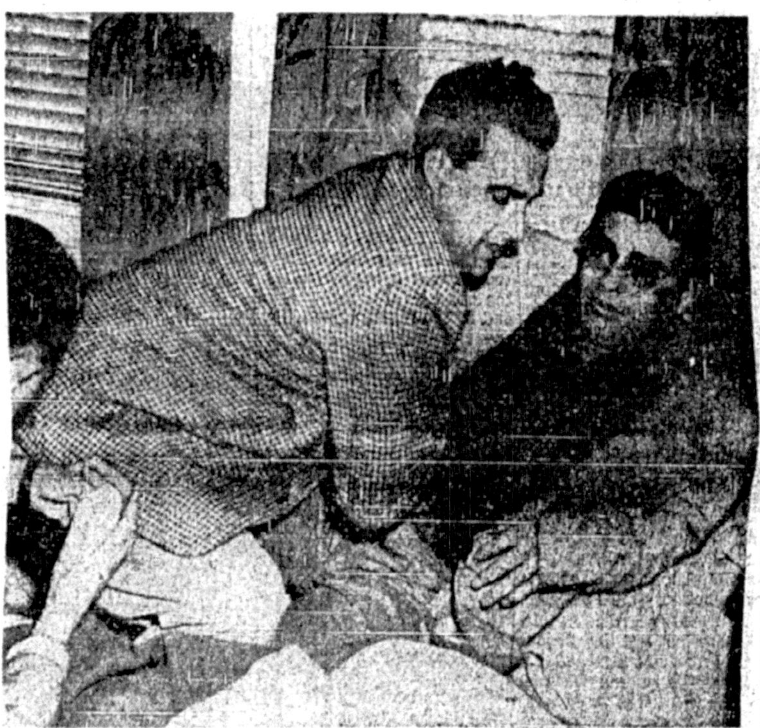

Christopher De Ollas was a major heroin dealer in the Tenderloin until the police arrested him in 1957 by setting up a buy in a drug agent's hotel room on the corner of Eddy and Jones streets. Drugs and drug dealing have been a factor in Tenderloin life since at least the 1890s. [*San Francisco Examiner*]

By the time this photograph was taken in 1958, most of the NBC Radio City building was rented out and NBC's music programming was mostly recorded. In addition, large development projects such as the Downtown Center Garage (shown here next to Radio City) and clearance for the Hilton Hotel (the empty lots across from Radio City and the garage) were causing the demolition of many inexpensive residential hotels. [*San Francisco History Center/San Francisco Public Library*]

Another example of the Tenderloin as a growth opportunity in the early 1950s to late 1960s was Sam's Original Brauhaus on the northwest corner of Mason and Turk streets (now the Hotel Bijou). In this 1964 photograph, it's around lunch time and the streets are crowed with people looking for somewhere to eat. This amount of legitimate sidewalk traffic started fading in the late 1960s and has never returned. [*Courtesy of Alan L. Canterbury/San Francisco History Center/San Francisco Public Library*]

With the construction and planning of at least eleven development projects between 1951 and 1968, the economic prognosis for the Tenderloin looked good enough for Bank of America to open two branches there. One (shown here) was built in 1960 on the corner of Golden Gate Avenue and Hyde streets, while the other was built on Ellis Street between Mason and Taylor in 1963, just half a block from Glide Church and across the street from the Hilton Hotel project. [*San Francisco History Center/San Francisco Public Library*]

In 1960, the northern edge of the Tenderloin along O'Farrell and Geary streets was still relatively prosperous when compared to the rest of the district. At the corner of Geary and Taylor streets there was the Clift Hotel with its Redwood Room next door to two of San Francisco's stage theaters. But by this time the Bellevue and the Maryland, the two other hotels sharing the corner with the Clift, had become inexpensive residential hotels occupied largely by seniors. [*Western Neighborhoods Project/Private collector*]

Eddie Skolak's President Follies, the last of the traditional burlesque theaters in San Francisco, closed in 1963 after his death. A *San Francisco Chronicle* reporter wrote, "Hundreds of outraged burlesque patrons hammered on the doors of San Francisco's famed old President Follies last night in a frenzy to see the final show. Inside, a standing-room only crowd of 1,100 shouted their appreciation as the strippers went through their last routine."[2] The old theater was offered for sale, and the Actor's Workshop lost out to a better offer from St. Boniface Church, just in back of the building. St. Boniface's original plan was to build a ten-story building on the site and conduct religious services there twenty-four hours a day, seven days a week. But the financing didn't work out and it was demolished and transformed into a parking lot until the 1980s when the Dorothy Day Community senior housing project was built on the site. [*San Francisco History Center/San Francisco Public Library*]

Starting in 1963, the building on the right was listed as an X-rated movie theater called the Gayety, which changed its spelling to Gaiety in 1978, apparently to clarify itself as a heterosexual business. In the 2000s it became the Dollhouse and in 2015 was remodeled into a theater space called CounterPulse. Next door, the storefront at 90 Turk Street in the Warfield Hotel was listed in 1974 as an escort service called The Play Girl, and the following year both 84 and 90 Turk were listed as an X-rated movie theater called the San Francisco Film Den. It morphed into Fantasy in Flesh (shown here in the 1980s), a business where the customer walked in, bought tokens from a clerk, and went to booths where he fed the tokens into a slot to keep an electronic sliding panel open while he talked to a naked woman through a plate glass window. [*shapingsanfrancisco*]

On June 19, 1964, President Johnson flew into San Francisco and motorcaded along Market Street and up Turk on his way to deliver the keynote address at the dedication of the New Federal Building on Golden Gate Avenue between Larkin and Polk during a fundraising swing through California. He must have seen the Hotel and Restaurant Workers, Musicians, and Ladies Garment Workers union signs because he stopped the motorcade and got out to press the flesh right there on the corner of Turk and Mason streets. That's California Congressman Phillip Burton in the foreground, with LBJ in the middle of the picture. [*Western Neighborhoods Project/Private collector*]

In 1965, Glide Church hired an outreach worker who encouraged both heterosexual and homosexual street people and hustlers to visit the church. In 1966, a group of ministers at the church helped start an organization they named Vanguard (not related to the now defunct charitable foundation with a similar name) as a way to agitate against the municipal and military police sweeps and arrests that were conducted in the Tenderloin as part of a drive to decrease the incidence of venereal disease among military troops during the Vietnam War. In this June 1966 photograph a group of demonstrators were symbolically protesting the sweeps. [*Foundsf*]

When Celso Ruperto bought the Sound of Music in 1977 or 1978, he changed the name to the Sound of Music Theatre and staged drag shows until 1979 or 1980, when he switched to punk rock. The club became famous as *the* place in San Francisco to perform if you were an unknown punk rocker: almost anyone could, and did, play there. [*Jeanne Hansen*]

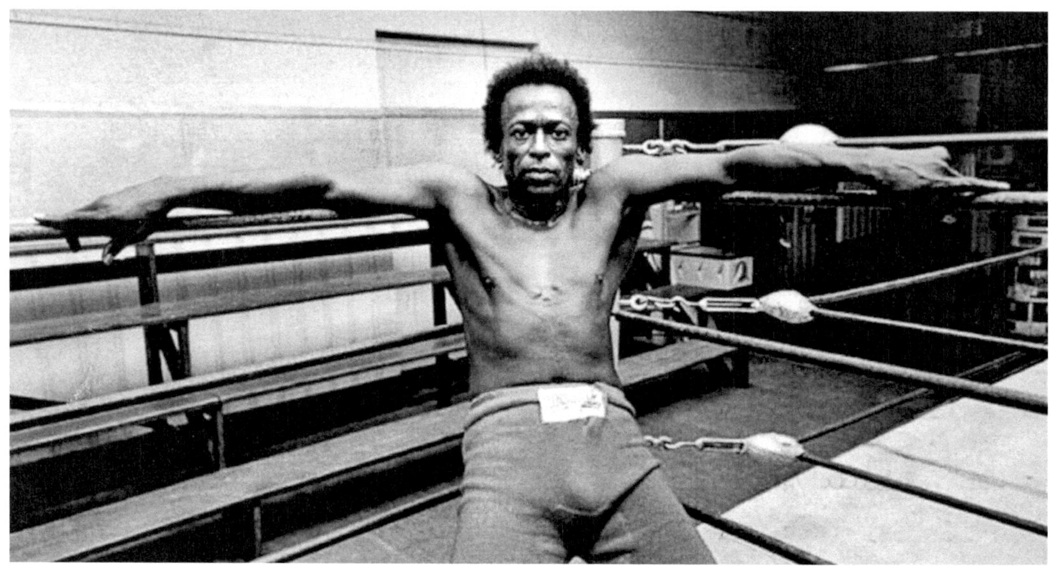

There was a boxing gym at 312 Leavenworth Street in one of the Cadillac Hotel storefronts since at least 1926, when Moose Taussig & Paddy Ryan opened it. Billy Newman took over around 1943 and ran it until his death forty years later. A number of famous boxers worked out there when they were in San Francisco, including Muhammad Ali when he was still Cassius Clay, as well as George Foreman and others. Jazz trumpeter Miles Davis also liked to spar wherever he was performing, and Newman's was where he'd go (shown here at Newman's in 1971) when he was playing in San Francisco. [*Jim Marshall*]

Jim and Artie Mitchell opened the O'Farrell Theatre in 1969 on the corner of O'Farrell and Polk streets as an X-rated movie venue. In 1972 they joined the new craze of making feature length, full color pornographic movies with decent production values, story lines, and acting (well, sort of) to attract mixed middle-class audiences. Their first effort, *Behind the Green Door*, became an X-rated hit after the star, Marilyn Chambers, told them weeks before the release that Ivory Soap had just taken a picture from a photo shoot two years before and used it to put her face on every box of Ivory soap as the Ivory Soap mom. Using the brand's widely known advertising slogan, the brothers spun this into a publicity campaign advertising Chambers as "99 and 44/100 percent impure." [*Author's collection*]

This building was erected in 1938 by architect William Gunnison for Local 48 of the Waitress' Union, which used the building until 1973. It was next occupied by the Bharativa Mandal Hall in 1974, an Indian community center on Ellis Street between Jones and Leavenworth. Why an Indian community center in the Tenderloin? Because many of the privately-operated SRO hotels in the Tenderloin and South of Market have been owned and operated by Indians, many of whom were named Patel. It still serves as a meeting hall and wedding hall and is used for other functions. [*Author's collection*]

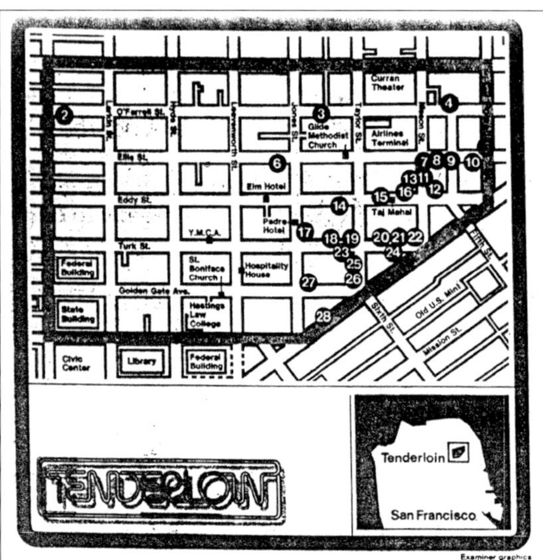

Who owns the 'adult' stores

The map and the list show where the Tenderloin's "adult" outlets are located, who has the permit on each and the owner of the property.

1. Powell Street News, bookstore and peep shows, 209 Powell St. Permit holder is Herb Kirat of Kentfield. Property owner is 207 Powell St. Ltd., a company headed by Ben Simon, who also has an adult book store at 101½ Powell.

2. O'Farrell Theatre, 895 O'Farrell, movies and live sex shows. Permit holder is Jim Mitchell, Tiburon, of the Mitchell Bros. Film Group. Property owner is Beatrice F. Presant of San Francisco.

3. O'Farrell Books & Novelties, 447 O'Farrell. Proprietor is William Ellery Jr. Property owners are William Auslen and Charles Gibbs Jr. of San Francisco.

4. The Sweet Shop, encounter parlor, 282 O'Farrell. Permit holder is Michael Musto, secretary of Ron London's Barone Amusement Co. Property owner is Ann Hamburger of San Francisco.

5. Ben Simon Book Co., 101½ Powell St. Proprietor is Ben Simon. Property owners are Burk H. and Mary Chung of San Francisco.

6. Ellis Adult Books, 415 Ellis. Proprietor is Howard Crenshaw. Property owners are Guey Thin Lee and Oy Bo Young, San Francisco.

7. Cupid's Corner, encounter parlor, 199 Ellis. Permit holder is Diane Heckenberg, a nurse at Kaiser Hospital in The City. Property owner is Tivoli Properties Inc., 870 Market, San Francisco, whose chief executive officer is Martin Hertz of the Hertz shoe repair family.

8. Mr. B's Books, 189 Ellis. Proprietor is Charles Harris of Burlingame. Property owned by Tivoli Properties Inc.

9. Love Nest, encounter parlor, 187 Ellis, currently closed. Permit holder is Gordon Grow of San Francisco. Property owner is Tivoli Properties Inc.

10. House of Joy, encounter parlor, 139 Ellis. Permit holder is Michael Musto of Barone Amusement Co. Property owners are Nicholas and Virginia Daphne of Hillsborough, who also own several San Francisco funeral parlors.

11. Spartan Theater, films and live male dancers, 150 Mason. Permit holder is Charles Harris of the Sun-Moon Corp., 75 Taylor, San Francisco. Property owner is Tivoli Properties Inc.

12. Pink Kat Arcade, books and peep movies, 142 Mason. Permit holder is Charles Harris, Burlingame. Property owner is Tivoli Properties.

13. Frenchy's K & T Books, 141 Mason. Permit holder is Earl S. Kuhns of San Francisco. Property owner is Ann Hamburger.

14. J & B Adult Book Shop, 233 Eddy. Proprietors are Ram Jalan and Fatima Bibi of San Francisco. Property owners are Thakor B. and Kamuben T. Desai of San Francisco.

15. The Tea Room, movie theater, 145 Eddy. Permit holder is Charles Harris of the Sun-Moon Corp. Property owners are Vasilios and Christine Glimidakis, of San Francisco, owners of the Minerva Cafe, 136 Eddy.

16. Adult Books, 110 Eddy. Proprietor is Robert Townsend of Berkeley. Property owner is Tuvia Volansky of San Francisco, who also owns McDonald's used book shop, 48 Turk.

17. The Screening Room, movie theater and live sex shows, 220 Jones. Permit holder is Kathryn A. Reed of San Francisco. Property owner is Alei DeRenzy of Novato, who has made several adult movies.

18. The Pleasure Palace, books and peep shows, 120 Turk. Permit holder is Jerald L. Thompson of San Rafael. Property owners are Gene N. and Jeanette L. Woo of San Francisco.

19. Frenchy's K & T Books, books and peep shows, 101 Taylor. Permit holder is Earl S. Kuhns of San Francisco. Property owners are Archie Schelfer and Friedman Investment Co.

20. San Francisco Film Den, movies, 90 Turk. Permit holder is Steven Waisman of San Francisco. Property owner is Title Insurance & Trust Co., 180 Pine St., San Francisco.

21. Gayety Theatre, movies, 80 Turk. Permit-holder is Peter A. DeCenzie, of Burlingame, who was the co-producer of the film "The Immoral Mr. Teas" and ran a number of burlesque shows in the 1950s and 1960s. Property owners are Louis and Josephine Rocca, of San Francisco, owners of Original Joe's restaurant.

22. Turk Street News, books and peep shows, 86 Turk. Permit holder is Jack A. Wolf of Pacifica. Property is held by trustee Henry Horn & Sons Real Estate and Insurance, 1833 Ocean Ave., San Francisco, for the estate of Marie Pappens.

23. Turk Street Follies, movies and live male dancers, 105 Turk. Permit holder is Harold A. Davis of Oakland. Property owners are Gilmer and Marjorie Anselmo and Frank M. Martino, all of San Francisco.

24. Palace Theater, live strip shows, 53 Turk. Permit holder is Harold A. Davis, Oakland. Property owners are Howard and Jean Cohn of San Rafael, owners of Maxferd Jewelry Co., 972 Market.

25. San Francisco Film Exchange, books and peep shows, 63 Taylor. Permit holder is William J. Pilchik, San Francisco. Property owners are Gilmer and Marjorie Anselmo and Frank M. Martino.

26. Art Theater, movies and peep shows, 55 Taylor. Permit holder is Herb Kirst of Kentfield. Property owners are Gilmer and Marjorie Anselmo and Frank M. Martino.

27. Mini-Adult Theater, movies, 96 Golden Gate Ave. Permit holder is Mark Johnson of Pacifica. Property owner is Jack Ben Sen Association, c/o Lowenberg Realty Co., 44 Montgomery, San Francisco.

28. Arcade Books and Movies, books and peep shows, 1034 Market. Permit holder is Delmar O. Seivers of San Francisco. Property is held by trustees Crocker National Bank and Antonio Romasanta for the estate of Marguerite Doe Ravenscroft.

Examiner graphics

In 1977, the *San Francisco Examiner* ran a week-long exposé of conditions in the Tenderloin. One of the things the paper reported was the existence of twenty-eight adult bookstores, massage parlors, and adult movie theaters in the neighborhood, almost all of them crowded into just five square blocks. One of the more surprising revelations was that the owner of an "encounter parlor" was a registered nurse at a local hospital. [*San Francisco Examiner*]

'We all have a different drummer,' says prosperous pornography vendor Earl Kuhns. Customers can pick up the rhythm in any of 45 peep show booths at Kuhns' Frenchy's K & T bookstore, where an early Linda Lovelace effort was recently a featured attraction.

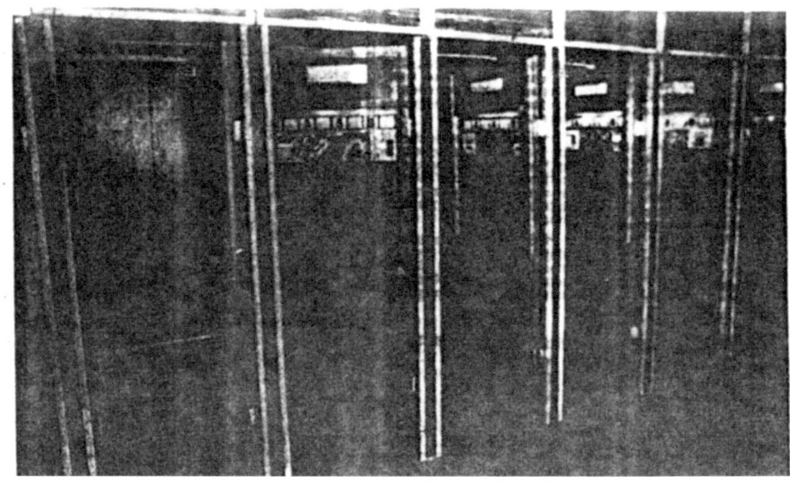

The *Examiner* exposé reported Earl Kuhns was one of the biggest owners of adult businesses in the Tenderloin. There was his flagship store on the northwest corner of Turk and Taylor streets (now ECI, a privately-operated jail and drug treatment program), another store on Mason Street (now the Hilton Hotel), and a third store on Geary Street between Polk and Van Ness (now a construction site for the UCSF downtown campus). He was eventually convicted of pimping—his female employees were offering sex for money in the stores' private booths. [*San Francisco Examiner*]

In 1977, former heroin addict Leroy Looper bought the rundown Cadillac Hotel on the northeast corner of Eddy and Leavenworth streets for his Reality House West nonprofit to rehab into housing for released convicts. Kathy Looper signed on as a social worker, fell in love with Looper, and married him. The Cadillac was the first modern subsidized hotel in San Francisco, following in the footsteps of Depression-era places like the nearby Evangeline Residence and the Mary Elizabeth Inn. [*Central City Hospitality House/Tenderloin Times*]

After 1975, Southeast Asian refugees began moving into the Tenderloin because of the cheap housing. They were generally families with children who crowded into studio apartments or hotel rooms, like the family in this photograph. [*Author's collection*]

Opposite page: The new immigrants did their best to preserve their cultural traditions in the new and strange environment. This is a Laotian Eu-mien hilltribe wedding ceremony in 1985. [*Central City Hospitality House/Tenderloin Times*]

Mien Wedding

Young dancers from the Eu-mien hilltribe in Laos at wedding festivities last month.

In a sign of the times, the neighborhood's oldest legitimate movie house, the Larkin Theatre, became the X-rated Century Theatre in 1979, which was then remodeled into the New Century in the 2000s. The latter two venues were strip club/lap dance/porno film houses. [*Author's collection*]

This photograph was taken in the lobby of a nameless Tenderloin hotel around 1981. By this time many seniors on limited incomes had lived in the Tenderloin for years, taking advantage of the inexpensive housing. As the neighborhood became less safe in the 1970s and 1980s, those who could afford to move out of the area did so. The ones who remained became easy victims for the predators that were moving into the Tenderloin. [*Greg Mancuso*]

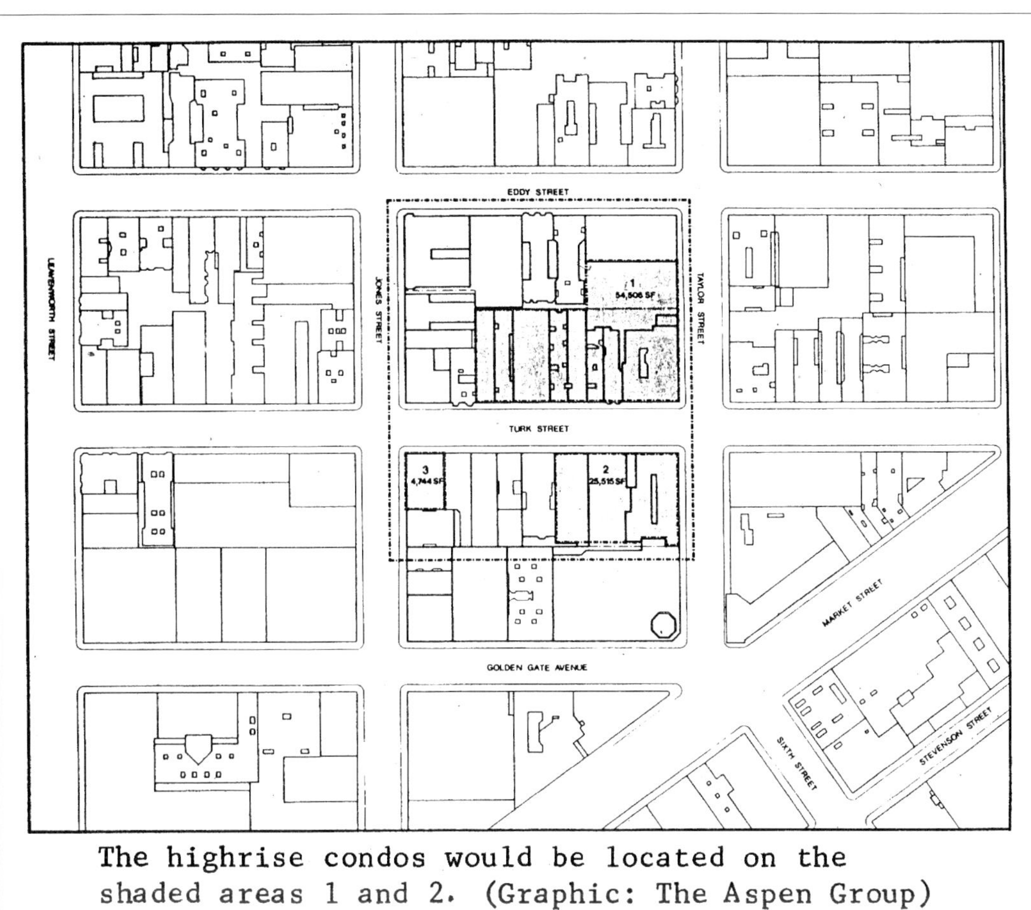

The highrise condos would be located on the shaded areas 1 and 2. (Graphic: The Aspen Group)

In 1981, a developer who had previously assembled a large real estate parcel for a high-rise tourist hotel, which resulted in knocking down five inexpensive residential hotels, claimed to have assembled another two parcels which would raze another nine inexpensive residential hotels and two inexpensive apartment buildings. Neighborhood activists forced him to defend his project to the San Francisco Planning Commission where it was discovered that not only did he not own the properties, he hadn't even gotten agreements to sell from most of the owners. [*Central City Hospitality House/Tenderloin Times*]

Opposite page: One of the Tenderloin's best-known residents in the 1980s and 1990s was an Emperor Norton-like character who called himself Cardinal Mahdi Mahatma Crown Prince Jesus Christ Satan, or just Crown Prince Arcadia as he was known to most people. Arcadia showed up at neighborhood and political meetings, providing occasional comic relief, like the time he suggested solving the homeless problem by placing huge cardboard tubes (normally used as concrete forms) at bus stops for the homeless to sleep in. [*Berkeley Barb*]

Aranda Tenants Win Heat Suit

Alice Fylstra, Lillian Beazly and Elizabeth Knight. They were the original Aranda tenants who brought the heat issue to the public's attention.

The Aranda Hotel, a residential SRO on Turk Street between Mason and Taylor, contracted with the Department of Social Services to rent rooms to welfare recipients. In December of 1982, residents complained about the hotel's substandard living conditions, the most serious of which was lack of heat. The North of Market Planning Coalition, a neighborhood advocacy group, and the Tenderloin Housing Clinic (THC), a tenant's rights organization, organized picket lines in front of some of the offending hotels. Randy Shaw, a young lawyer at THC, took *San Francisco Chronicle* columnist Warren Hinckle on a tour of Tenderloin hotel heating problems. Hinckle wrote an incendiary page-one feature-length story that started a firestorm of protest resulting in the city inspecting 130 hotels in seven days, with fifty cited for failing to meet heating codes. The ladies in the photograph are the three Aranda tenants who first initiated the complaints. [*Central City Hospitality House/Tenderloin Times*]

One of the Tenderloin's best kept secrets was Rasputin, a Russian restaurant and club in a storefront in the Alexander Residence, a nonprofit subsidized hotel on Eddy Street between Taylor and Jones. The main entrance was apparently through a back door leading from a parking lot on Ellis Street. [*Central City Hospitality House/Tenderloin Times*]

The Ramada Renaissance Hotel, the Hilton Hotel, and the Holiday Inn were required by an agreement hammered out with the city to donate funds to the neighborhood to mitigate the effects of their hotel projects on the area. In this 1984 photograph, Ramada Renaissance Hotel Manager John Small gave a $50,000 ceremonial check to longtime neighborhood activist Leroy Looper for distribution to Tenderloin projects. [*Central City Hospitality House/Tenderloin Times*]

THE TENDERLOIN

Police Crack Down on Prostitutes

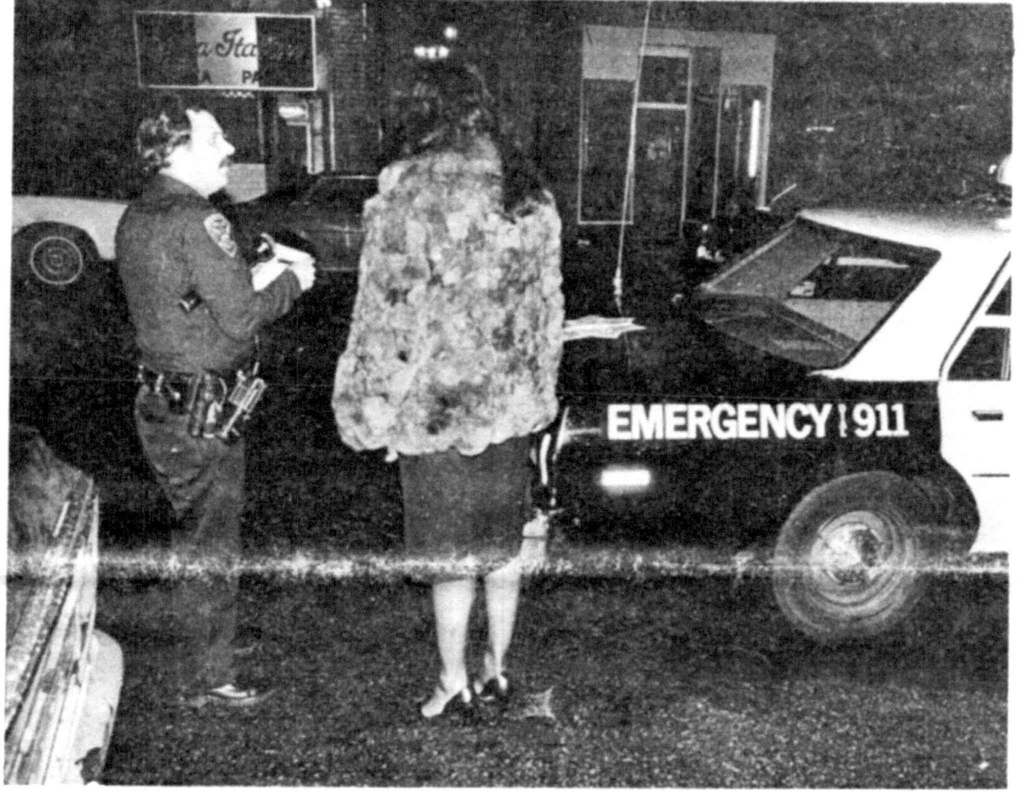

Police issuing ticket for ''obstructing the sidewalk.''   photo: Andrew Ritchie

The only thing that changed about prostitution in the Tenderloin was that after the 1960s it went onto the street ... where it still is today. The photo was taken in 1984. [*Central City Hospitality House/Tenderloin Times*]

toilet in Kaussen's King Edward apartments, 275 Turk. The City has filed suit against Kaussen for poor conditions there.

With street conditions steadily deteriorating, the Tenderloin started getting foot patrols by beat cops, as seen in this 1984 photo. [*Central City Hospitality House/Tenderloin Times*]

Opposite page: This 1984 photograph is of one of the bathrooms in the King Edward Apartments at 275 Turk Street between Jones and Leavenworth, one of several Tenderloin buildings owned by Guenter Kaussen. A German multimillionaire, his business model was to buy cheap, run-down buildings in economically run-down areas around the world, make superficial improvements, and then start jacking up rents. Much of this was done through illegal evictions. As the rents increased, so did the property values, and Kaussen would then get approval for loan amounts based on the buildings' artificially inflated worth instead of on their actual value. Many of his San Francisco tenants were elderly or disabled and on limited incomes. He was eventually sued and forced to divest himself of his San Francisco properties. [*Central City Hospitality House/Tenderloin Times*]

Two Views of Crime in the Tenderloin

Win Cottrell

Tom Finney

In 1985, retired nurse and Tenderloin housing activist Win Cottrell lived in a condo in the posh Hamilton on O'Farrell Street in the less crime-ridden north Tenderloin and felt safe. Nonprofit agency employee Tom Finney worked in the middle of the south Tenderloin and was beaten up twice near his job, prompting him to quit. It was this sort of thing that led to a neighborhood split between people who wanted to protect civil liberties and people who wanted more law enforcement to make the streets safe. [*Central City Hospitality House/Tenderloin Times*]

Opposite above: In 1985, Mayor Dianne Feinstein signed a measure making permanent the rezoning of the Tenderloin into a residential neighborhood with a 120-foot height limit. The purpose was to halt three decades of big development projects that caused the demolition of dozens of inexpensive residential hotels and apartment buildings and drove up housing costs. This level of development was one of the economic trends that set the stage for the homeless epidemic, in this case by reducing the number of cheap residential housing units while increasing the cost of the ones that were left. [*Central City Hospitality House/Tenderloin Times*]

Feinstein Signs Tenderloin Rezoning

Neighborhood leaders turned rezoning petition over to City Planning officials in 1981. Four years and some compromises later, it's law. Pictured from left: Leroy Looper, Rev. Cecil Williams, Father Robert Pfisterer, Planning Director Dean Macris, Commissioner Sue Bierman, Deputy Planning Director Robert Passmore.

Photo: Sara Colm

by Sara Colm

Mayor Feinstein officially signed

Macris with maps and documents officially proposing the rezoning change, which went into effect im-

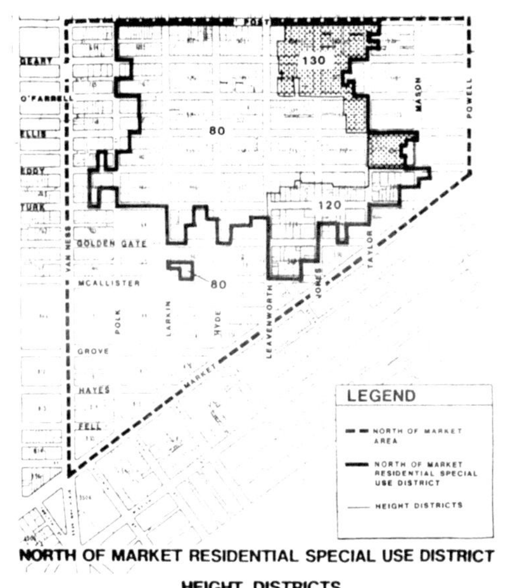

Boeddeker Park, the neighborhood's second (shown here), was opened in 1985 on the old Downtown Bowl site on the northeast corner of Eddy and Jones streets, directly across from the office of the North of Market Planning Coalition, an advocacy agency that had done much to help lead the effort to build it. Unfortunately, neighborhood advocates' wishes for a non-fenced in park prevailed over neighborhood residents' demands for a more security-conscious design, and so it became a hangout for drinkers and street people. Despite the problems, the presence of a recreation center with a recreation director helped ensure the park's activities for children stayed in place. It took an expensive makeover in 1998 and a very expensive rebuilding in 2014 to safety proof Boeddeker Park for everyone. The photograph shows the park before its redesign. [*Author's collection*]

Theology in Practice—on the Streets of the Tenderloin

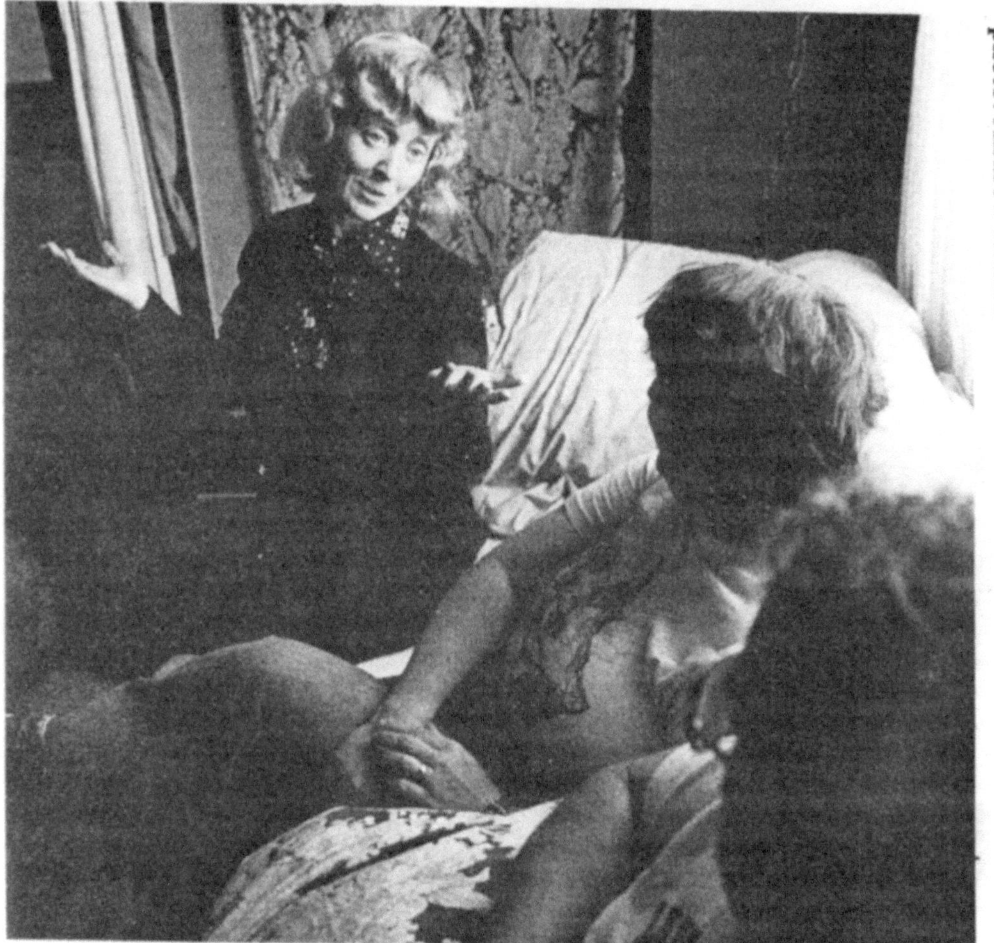

The Rev. Glenda Hope visits with Ray Greenwood and Yvonne Elam in their Ambassador Hotel room.

Reverend Glenda Hope, a diminutive pastor who grew up in the South and was a civil rights activist, worked in the Tenderloin beginning in 1981 for about thirty-two years. In that time, she started or helped start "house churches" in Tenderloin hotels; conducted memorials for deceased Tenderloin residents (both the homeless and the housed); conducted hotel ministries for AIDS sufferers; organized Tenderloin AIDS services (when there were none to be had); organized a large housing project for low income families; started a computer education and repair service for Tenderloin residents; and started a housing program for prostitutes trying to get out of The Life. In this 1985 photograph she's visiting two residents of the Ambassador Hotel. [*Central City Hospitality House/Tenderloin Times*]

Richard Gaule opened Soups on O'Farrell Street between Hyde and Larkin (now the Stop & Save Market) in late 1991 where he served a big bowl of thick soup with crackers for a very low price and offered a free refill. About ten years before, Gaule came to the Tenderloin flat broke and learned how to get along with Tenderloin residents by managing cheap residential hotels like the Elk and the Balboa. He operated Soups until he died in 2005. [*Author's collection*]

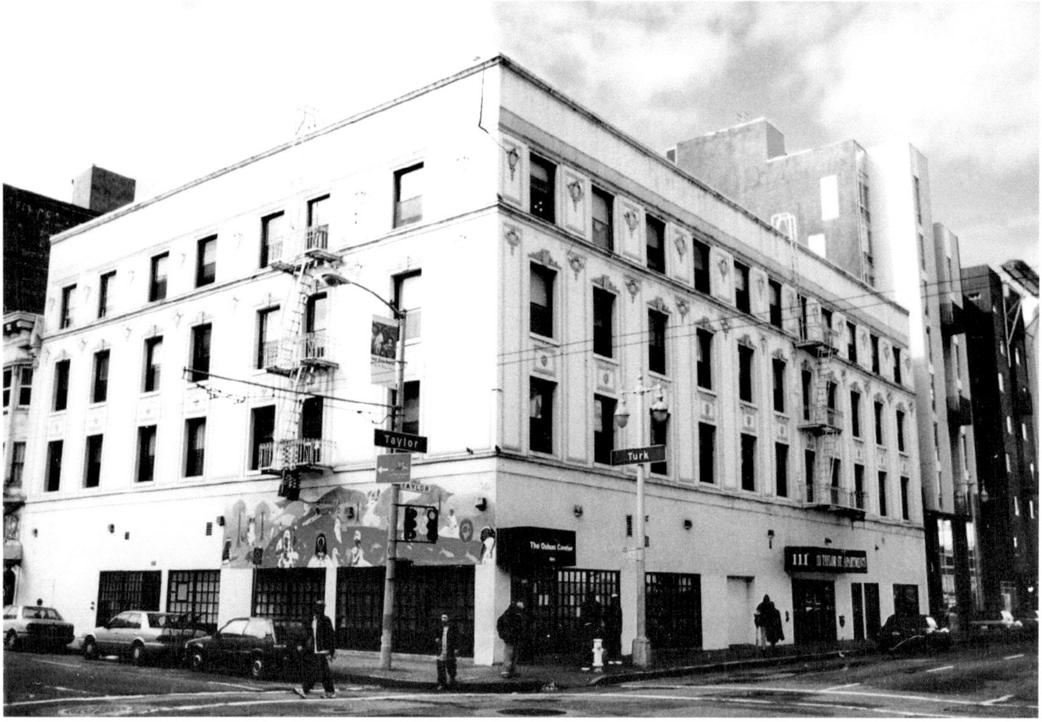
Taylor
Turk
The Oshun Center
111

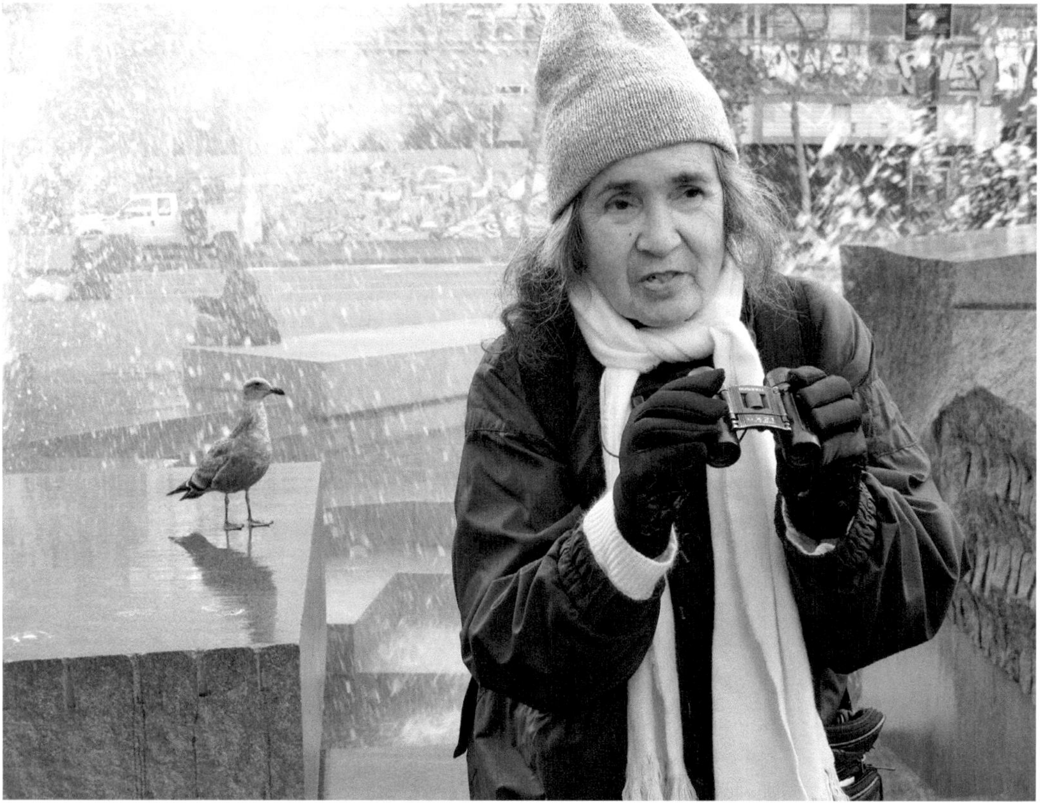

Above: According to architectural historians Ann Bloomfield and Michael Corbett, the Hotel Clark got a new Moderne look in 1950, which it retains today (photo taken around 2010). The building now houses the Tenderloin Neighborhood Development Corporation's offices and the Franciscan Towers, a TNDC subsidized housing project. [*Author's collection.*]

Opposite above: There was good news in 1989 for the corner of Turk and Taylor streets when the Hyland Hotel, which had been closed for a decade after a fire made the residential floors uninhabitable, was remodeled into an inexpensive residential SRO hotel. But in 1993, an innocuously named company, Eclectic Communications, Inc., leased the entire building and remodeled it into one of its private jails and drug treatment programs, despite protests from neighborhood groups. It still operates at that location. [*Author's collection*]

Opposite below: Mary Liz Harris and her husband Richard were longtime Tenderloin residents who lived in the Piedmont Apartments at 270 Turk Street between Jones and Leavenworth (now the Barcelona Apartments). Every winter she did the neighborhood bird counts for the Audubon Society's annual census. She ragged the author for years about offering his City Guides Tenderloin history walking tours only on Sunday mornings. City Guides finally got them to schedule a private tour with the author and she and her group of fellow seniors turned out to be from a local Church of Latter-Day Saints congregation who couldn't go on the Sunday morning tours because it would have meant missing Sunday services. Even their young bishop and his wife came along. [*Tom Carter/Central City Extra*]

In 2018 (see above photo) the Warfield Hotel on the northeast corner of Taylor and Turk streets has a new paint job and a new bar named Biig, which replaced the 21 Club, a longtime neighborhood watering hole in the corner storefront when the owner retired. The new bar has no signage, the entrance is locked, and the only way to get in is to make online reservations and knock on the door upon arrival. The owner says they're getting enough business to pay their employees, but street conditions in the neighborhood keep many potential customers away. The former SRO residential hotel upstairs has been extensively renovated and is now operated as tourist lodgings, even though it's directly across the street from a privately-operated jail and drug program. [*Author's collection*]

This building at 540 Leavenworth Street between O'Farrell and Geary, recently rehabbed into the Element Apartments, has gotten a trendy face lift. But a close look shows it's designed to make it hard for unauthorized people to get into the building, impossible for the homeless to sleep in the entranceway, and difficult to graffiti. [*Author's collection*]

The Hotel Verona at 301 Leavenworth Street on the northwest corner of Eddy has recently acquired a new tenant—the Black Cat bar in the corner storefront space. Like many of the new Tenderloin businesses, the frontage is designed to discourage unwanted attention from street people and to make enough money to survive until conditions improve to the point that customers will start coming into the Tenderloin again. [*Author's collection*]

One of the groups that has figured out how to make it in the Tenderloin are the Southeast Asian immigrants that flooded the neighborhood in the late 1970s and 1980s. With a customer base of neighborhood residents as a foundation, the addition of a relatively small number of visitors hardy enough to brave the area are enough for the businesses, largely restaurants, to show a profit. [*Author's collection*]

ENDNOTES

1. "Mason Street Shoeshiner Reflects on Tenderloin's Soul," *Tenderloin Times*, February 1990, 14.
2. "A Frenzied Final Night at the Follies," *San Francisco Chronicle*, September 6, 1963, 1.

THE TENDERLOIN TODAY

In the nineteenth century, the Tenderloin had between had between ten and twenty churches, three public schools and a number of private schools, and a large stock of family housing. There were many families with children living there, even during the district's first decades as a hotel, entertainment, and vice district. Generally speaking, it was a prosperous area. After the 1906 earthquake and fire, it had just three churches, one public school, and little family housing. Relatively few families with children lived there. In 1944 there were so few families that the Tenderloin's one remaining public school closed. After the Korean War, the the area slowly slid into poverty.

In the 1980s the families and the children came back—thousands of them. They were mostly Southeast Asian refugees, welfare recipients, and undocumented Spanish speakers. Now there are just two churches, but there is also a new public school and two private schools. There are four parks. There are also any number of programs and agencies to help families. The typical Tenderloin family lives in a studio apartment unless they're fortunate enough to have gotten into one of the limited number of subsidized family housing developments.

The neighborhood itself is anything but a family neighborhood, filled with street homeless, drug addicts, alcoholics, criminals, and the physically and mentally disabled. There are few family-oriented businesses. There are many bars, clubs, massage parlors, sex clubs, corner grocery and liquor stores, and hotels. Not an environment for children. Yet the children are there.

As of 2018, when this is being written, the area has improved in some ways. There are fewer sleaze bars, far fewer X-rated businesses, and fewer corner liquor stores. Several of the blocks that were notorious for their street activity are now largely emptied of street people since the demolition of buildings and the businesses that attracted trouble were replaced with modern subsidized housing. There are frequent news reports about these improvements. Former San Francisco Mayor and State Assembly Speaker Willie Brown comments on them frequently in his weekly *San Francisco Chronicle* column. There are now homeless services in other neighborhoods besides the Tenderloin and South of Market, and they are starting to get some people off the streets.

But there are also frequent news reports about all the street activity that hasn't gone away, shifting from location to nearby location. Many blocks are still bad, the streets are still filthy, and much of the neighborhood still looks run down. The street homeless, panhandlers, acting-out mentally ill, drug addicts, and drunks still make the neighborhood unapproachable to most people. There is still much crime. Because of these things, new businesses still have a hard time attracting enough customers to make a profit.

What's the next step?

Peter Field is a retired San Francisco and San Mateo County homeless mental health case manager who is also an historian and author who leads walking history tours of the city's Tenderloin and Richmond districts.